Home Improvements and Conversions

Home Improvements and Conversions

Timber Research and Development Association

THE CONSTRUCTION PRESS

LANCASTER   LONDON   NEW YORK

The Construction Press Ltd,
Lancaster, England.

A subsidiary company of Longman Group Ltd, London.
Associated companies, branches and representatives
throughout the world.

Published in the United States of America by
Longman Inc, New York.

First published 1978

ISBN 0 86095 811 6

Printed in Great Britain at The Pitman Press, Bath.

Contents

PUBLISHERS NOTE

This book has been compiled from a series of publications originally prepared by Peter Knowles RIBA as part of a major study undertaken by the Timber Research and Development Association (TRADA) for the Department of the Environment. The contents cover a range of problems that may be encountered in home improvement work.

Each section makes reference to and takes account of The Building Regulations (1976) operative throughout England and Wales except for the inner London Boroughs of the Greater London Council. Much of the advice given is equally applicable in Scotland and Northern Ireland but their respective Regulations differ slightly in contents and layout so that the regulation numbers or references given would not be directly applicable.

ACKNOWLEDGEMENT

We have pleasure in acknowledging the cooperation of TRADA in granting us permission to publish their material in this volume. Layout is by Trevor Tredwell AIPtgM (TRADA) and drawings are by Tim Wheeler, Henley-on-Thames.

Introduction to home improvements and conversions

'Home improvements and conversions' can range from redecoration of a single room to a major scheme designed to convert a row of houses into flats or maisonettes.

The series of leaflets of which this is the first were prepared by Peter Knowles, RIBA as part of a major study undertaken by TRADA for the Department of the Environment. The leaflets cover a range of problems that may be encountered in home improvement work.

This leaflet briefly discusses local authority improvement grants and how the Building Regulations affect work carried out in improving or converting a house into flats or maisonettes. More detailed reference is made to the Building Regulations in the succeeding leaflets. The interpretations are those of TRADA and reference should be made to the Regulations themselves and approval obtained from the local authority before work begins.

LOCAL AUTHORITY GRANTS

Grants of various types can be made by local authorities towards the cost of:

— providing dwellings by the conversion of houses and other buildings.

— improving dwellings.

— repairing dwellings.

— improving houses in multiple occupation by the provision of standard amenities.

The types of grant are:

— 'Improvement grant' which is available at the discretion of the local authority for the provision of a dwelling or for the improvement of a dwelling. After completion of the relevant works the dwelling must: be provided with the standard amenities for the exclusive use of the occupants, be in good repair and be likely to provide satisfactory housing accommodation for 30 years. The 'relevant limit of expenditure' is normally £3200 for a dwelling improved by the relevant works and £3700 for dwellings provided by conversion of a house or other building of 3 or more storeys. In all cases the house undergoing improvement must have been erected before 2nd October, 1961.

— 'Intermediate grant'; normally obtainable as of right to improve a dwelling by providing the standard amenities it lacks. After completion of the work, the dwelling should provide the full standard amenities, be in good repair and conform to the current thermal insulation requirements. It should be likely to be available for use as a dwelling for 15 years. The 'eligible expense' for works of repair or replacement is a maximum of £800, and £700 for provision of standard amenities.

— 'Special grant' for the improvement of a house in multiple occupation by the provision of the standard amenities is available at the local authority's discretion.

— 'Repairs grant' available at the local authority's discretion for repair of a dwelling in a housing action area or a general improvement area. This is paid only if the local authority believes the work could not be carried out without undue hardship to the applicant. The dwelling must attain a relevant standard of repair after the work. The grant paid is an 'appropriate percentage' of the 'eligible expense' and depends upon where the dwelling is situated:

— in a housing action area, maximum 75 per cent

— in a general improvement area, maximum 60 per cent

— in any other area, maximum 50 per cent

Provision of standard amenities

	Max eligible amount £
Fixed bath or shower	100
Hot and cold water supply at a fixed bath or shower	140
Wash-hand basin	50
Hot and cold water supply at wash-hand basin	70
Sink	100
Hot and cold water supply at sink	90
WC	150

When the improvement or conversion work is completed a dwelling must:

1 Be substantially free from damp

2 Have adequate natural lighting and ventilation in each habitable room

3 Have adequate and safe provision throughout for artificial lighting, and have sufficient electric socket outlets for the safe and proper functioning of domestic appliances

4 Be provided with adequate drainage facilities

5 Be in a stable structural condition

6 Have satisfactory internal arrangement

7 Have satisfactory facilities for preparing and cooking food

8 Be provided with adequate facilities for heating

9 Have proper provision for the storage of fuel (where necessary) and for the storage of refuse

10 Conform with the specifications applicable to the thermal insulation of roof spaces laid down in Part F of the Building Regulations in force at the date of the grant approval.

APPLICATION OF THE BUILDING REGULATIONS (ENGLAND AND WALES)

This information is for general guidance only. Detailed reference should be made to the Building Regulations.

In general the Building Regulations only apply to improvement work when structural alterations or extensions are involved. The Regulations always apply, however, if a single-family house (designated as Purpose Group I) is converted into flats or maisonettes (Purpose Group III) since this constitutes a 'change of use'.

It is not practical to require old buildings to comply with the modern Building Regulations, so a distinction is made between 'new work' which must comply, and the 'existing' which need not. Alterations or extensions to an existing building constitute new work. However, it is required that all 'existing' elements of the building which remain after the new work is carried out shall not contravene the Regulations more than they did before.

In the case of a house (PG I) being converted for occupation by two or more families (PG III) the existing must comply with the following Regulations:

Part E — 'Structural fire precautions' with the exception of
E7 External walls
E9(7) Compartment walls and compartment floors
E10(4) Protected shafts
E13 Stairways
E15 Restriction of surface flamespread over walls and ceilings.

Part J   Refuse disposal

Part K — 'Open space, ventilation and height of habitable rooms' with the exception of
K3 Zones of open space
K8 Height of habitable rooms.

Part L — 'Chimneys, fluepipes, hearths and fireplace recesses' with the exception of
L4(1)(c)(ii) and L4(1)(d)
L6 chimneys for class I appliances
L14 chimneys for class II appliances.

The following Regulations therefore DO NOT APPLY TO THE EXISTING when alterations and/or extensions take place:

Part B Materials
Part C Preparation of site and resistance to moisture
Part D Structural stability
Part F Thermal insulation
Part G Sound insulation
Part H Stairways and balustrades
Part M Heat producing appliances & incinerators
Part N Drainage, private sewers and cesspools
Part P Sanitary conveniences

Definitions

'CHANGE OF USE'. Alterations and/or extensions which change a building from one purpose group to another (eg from a private house into flats).

'NO CHANGE OF USE'. Alterations and/or extensions which do not change the purpose group.

PG I BUILDING. (Purpose Group I) 'Small Residential': a private house for single family occupation.

PG III BUILDING. (Purpose Group III) 'Other Residential': flats, bedsitters, maisonettes, hotel bedrooms, but not institutional buildings:

A FLAT is a single storey dwelling within a larger building. (Two or more flats are served by a 'common' stair).

A BEDSITTER is a small flat.

A MAISONETTE is a 2-storey dwelling within a larger building. (Two or more maisonettes are served by a 'common' stair, but the stair inside each maisonette is a 'private' stair).

Exercise of power of dispensation or relaxation

Application can be made to the local authority on the official form (as in schedule 4 of the Regulations) to dispense with or relax any of the regulations B to P except D — structural stability (Regulation A13 refers).

Relaxation of Part E — structural fire precautions can be applied for in the case of a PG I building or a change of use from PG I to PG III (Regulation A9(i) case B refers).

Building Regulations and Improvement Grants

Some items covered by the discretionary Improvement Grant have the effect of upgrading the existing to comply with the appropriate Building Regulation. (eg prevention of rising damp — Part C, or improvement of natural light and ventilation into a room — Part K).

It is also very desirable that sound insulation should be provided between flats when a PG I building is converted into PG III. Part G does not apply at the present time.

Applications for Improvement Grants, and Town Planning and Building Regulations approval, must be submitted to the local authority on the official forms. Work cannot start until full approval is given, for the first two of these and it would be unwise to start without approval of the third for if the work then done does not comply with the Regulations will have to be altered so that it does.

Mortgage. The building society's approval is required for any proposed structural alteration to a private house which is mortgaged.

Loans for home improvements from the local authority, or from a building society, are eligible for income tax relief on the interest repayments.

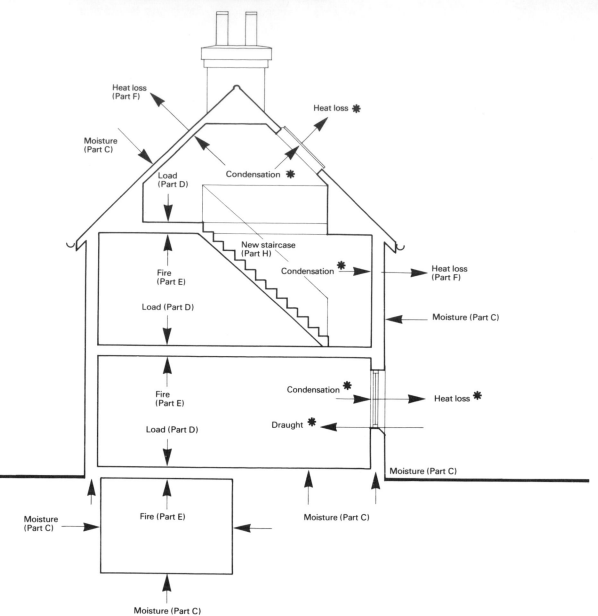

This section through a house shows the factors which should be considered in House Improvements. The Building Regulations govern all *new work* under the parts shown in brackets, but do not apply to existing areas which are not altered structurally — unless any new work adjacent has an adverse effect on the existing. Items marked ✳ are not included in the Building Regulations in England and Wales at present, (although heat loss through windows is included in Scotland). However, condensation might affect the durability of materials (Part B) and structural stability (Part D). In any case condensation, draughts and heat loss through windows should be dealt with, in order to improve comfort and reduce heating bills.

DAMPNESS

— reduces the effectiveness of insulation materials

— causes mould-growth on wallpaper, curtains, carpets, lino etc

— corrodes metals

— causes plaster or mortar to crumble

— encourages fungus-attack on timber.

Parts B and C of the Building Regulations are intended to prevent dampness occurring in new houses and in structural alterations or extensions to old houses, and such work must comply with the Building Regulations. A 'discretionary' Improvement Grant can be obtained to make the house 'substantially free from damp'.

SOURCES OF DAMPNESS — (fig 1)

1 RISING DAMP
2 CONDENSATION
3 PENETRATION FROM OUTSIDE
4 BUILT-IN MOISTURE

It is important to identify the source of dampness, as the remedies are different.

The simplest general remedy is good ventilation and heating: moisture will evaporate into the room and then to the outside through open windows. Furniture and floor coverings should be moved away from the damp area. This is a temporary solution only, since it makes the room unusable and wastes heat. Permanent remedies are listed below:

1 RISING DAMP from the ground is noticeable at skirting level, on walls in ground floor rooms, and on solid ground floors (fig 2). Where the ground floor is suspended timber it is essential to ventilate the space underneath with airbricks or plastics vents in the external wall (fig 3). The first step is to remove plants and soil from against the external wall. This will reduce the amount of moisture retained against the wall and will increase the exposed area from which evaporation can take place (fig 4). If rising damp persists a damp proof course (dpc) can be added if there is none already. It should be pointed out, however, that a good deal of money can be wasted in unnecessary installation of dpc's when there is little (or even no) rising damp or it occurs in only a small area. Houses built before 1875 were not required by law to have a dpc. Even if there is a dpc the ground level may have been built up with paving, and this often results in rainwater splashing off the hard paved surface onto the wall above the dpc. Ground level adjacent to the wall should be at least 150 mm (6 in) below the dpc.

There are several methods of adding a damp proof course:

a Mechanical A continuous slot (in short sections) is cut through the wall with a power saw, and then a metal or plastic dpc inserted. The work is noisy and unsuitable for rubble walls. It is economic only for walls of 9 in thickness or less.

● Specialists: Dampcoursing Ltd
          MDC Group Services 'Aridex' dpc
          Rentokil Ltd 'Discovac' dpc
The dpc must extend over the full thickness of the wall, otherwise damp may rise through the mortar joint.

b Electro-osmosis principle is a popular method, easier to install than (a). A 9 mm wide copper strip is set into a mortar joint at normal dpc level and connected to a copperclad earth-rod driven 4 to 6 m into the adjacent soil. The only visible evidence is a small bronze junction box on the wall face. The thickness and material of the wall present no obstacle to the use of this process.

● Specialists: Rentokil Ltd —
          'Electro-osmotic dampproofing'

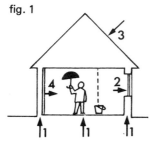

fig. 1

fig. 2

damp

fig. 3

vent

fig. 4

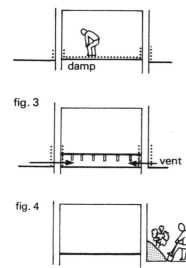

c Chemical injection involves drilling holes into the wall (from outside on an external wall) and feeding in water-proofing chemicals which permeate the wall material. This method is equally suitable for internal walls and basements, and the wall thickness and type of material presents no problem.

● Specialists: Cambridge Timberproofing Laboratories
                'ACTANE' injection
                Dampcoursing Ltd
                MDC Group Services — 'SPI'
                Nubold Ltd — 'Nubex'
                Peter Cox Ltd
                *Protim Knapen Gallwey Ltd
                Romanite DPC — No 132
                Preservation Development (1972) Ltd
                — 'Vandex' injection mortar
                Solignum Ltd — 'Impervion'
                Wykamit 'DPC' & 'PI'

Notes
● These lists are not comprehensive. The firms included offer a nationwide service; in addition there are locally-based firms who carry out such work. The method chosen will depend on the advice given by the specialists and on relative costs.

* In addition, porous clay siphon tubes are inserted into the wall at or above floor level, to increase evaporation to the outside.

Waterproofing the outside of an exposed external wall (see Section 3 below), if there is no dpc (fig 5) will prevent rising damp from evaporating to the outside and so increases dampness inside the house. (Silicone resins, however, have the advantage of preventing moisture penetration from the outside whilst permitting evaporation of moisture through the resin from the inside).

Solid ground floors should have a damp proof 'membrane' continuous with the wall dpc. Note, however, that what appears to be rising damp may be condensation on a solid floor (see Section 2 below). External waterproofing, eg rendering, should not extend below the dpc (fig 6). The 'membrane' can take the form of polythene sheeting or bituminous compound brushed onto a solid slab and covered with a sand and cement screed (at least 37 mm (1½ in) thick). Alternatively the screed can contain a waterproof additive, although this is not foolproof; an asphalt sub-floor can be laid with more success.

Screeds are wet and messy to put down, and require weeks to dry out. They can be eliminated by laying concrete tiles or clay tiles direct onto the membrane, but this requires a smooth and level base.

Existing timber suspended ground floors should be examined by taking up the floorboards. Rising damp in an unventilated space encourages rot (see 'Dampness in timber' p 9). If there is any sign of dry rot then all infected timbers should be removed and burnt. All sound timber within the room should be treated with a preservative in-situ. Sterilise plaster and brickwork also.

Reconstruction of the floor should be as follows (fig 7). Any topsoil should be cleared away and a thin layer of hardcore or gravel put down with a blinding layer of sand on top, pressed or rolled flat. On top of this should be laid a membrane of 500 gauge polythene sheet with joints overlapped at least 100 mm (4 in) and held down by heaps of sand. The gap between the membrane and the underside of the floor joists should

fig. 5 cross-section

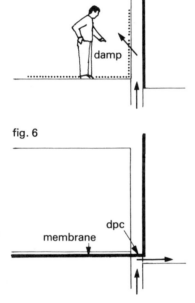

damp

fig. 6

dpc

membrane

fig. 7   detail cross-section (minimum dimensions shown)

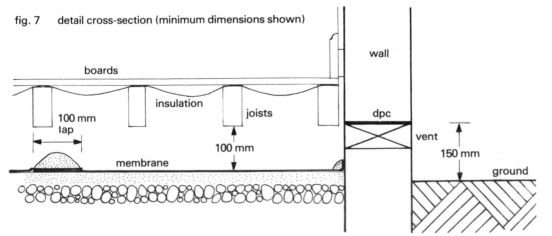

be at least 100 mm (4 in). Airbricks or plastics vents should be put through the external walls to give cross ventilation under the floor. Timber in contact with brickwork should be protected by a dpc. New timbers used in the floor should be preservative treated by pressure impregnation.

The membrane should be at or above external ground level. Where there is sufficient depth to carry out these recommendations a suspended timber floor has certain advantages over a solid concrete floor:

— speed

— dry construction

— no drying out period

— thermal insulation

the 'U' value of 25 mm (1 in) t & g softwood boarding over a vertical space is 0.69.

This can be further improved by incorporating insulation eg mineral wool quilt, or impregnated insulating board beneath the boards.

— warm and resilient to stand or sit on.

2 CONDENSATION FROM INSIDE

This problem is becoming more widespread as heating standards are improved, room ventilation is reduced, and more hot water is used in the house (fig 8).

The worst effects are on windows, on the upper part of external walls and under ceilings in the roof space. Condensation can also occur on solid ground floors and on internal walls if one room is heated and the adjoining room or house is cold.

Old houses are usually well ventilated (ie draughty) with large unheated rooms. There is no condensation problem until improvements are made, such as:

— draught strips fixed to doors and windows

— chimneys sealed up

— central heating installed

— hot water supply to bath, wash basin and sink

— large rooms sub-divided into small rooms.

The result of such improvements is to increase the quantity of water vapour in the atmosphere due to the higher room temperatures and the reduced ventilation.

Water vapour is produced by people when they breathe, (about two pints per person per day), perspire, wash, cook, bathe, dry clothes etc. Paraffin and gas heaters produce large amounts of water vapour. Warm air can hold more water vapour than cold air:

at 68°F, 33 cu yds of atmosphere contains 1 lb of water;
at 48°F, 33 cu yds of atmosphere contains $\frac{1}{2}$ lb of water.
} at 100 per cent relative humidity

When the air is saturated (100 per cent relative humidity) it can contain no more water vapour.

Condensation point is reached when either more water vapour is added, or when warm air is cooled (usually by a cold surface); the excess water vapour condenses into liquid water. The problem is greatest in winter but can occur during the summer if there is a sudden drop in temperature.

The first step in reducing condensation is to reduce the amount of water vapour in the atmosphere:

— by not using unflued paraffin heaters

— by avoiding prolonged boiling of kettles and pans

— by opening windows to let the water vapour escape.

An electric extractor fan is recommended in a kitchen, especially in an open-plan house: it will discharge water vapour to the outside without letting in cold air.

The daily pattern of occupation can effect condensation: if a house is empty throughout the day with the heating switched off, then it will be cold when people return in the evening and put the heating on, use hot water for washing and do their cooking. The rapid rise in temperature and relative humidity will produce condensation on cold surfaces — particularly with materials which have high thermal capacity (and therefore take a long time to warm up) such as brick, stone and

fig. 8 cross-section

concrete. Materials which have low thermal capacity on the other hand, such as wood and insulating boards, respond to heat very quickly and so the risk of condensation is reduced.

The permanent solution to condensation is a combination of heat, ventilation and good insulation (**See thermal insulation chapter**).
However, it is possible for water vapour to pass through the insulation and to condense on the inner face of the cold material, or even inside its thickness. (Water vapour is a gas under pressure which can pass through most building materials). Water produced in this situation will be absorbed by the insulating material and thus make it useless.

A vapour check should be put in to prevent this. It can be:
— polythene sheet
— aluminium foil
— building paper faced both sides with foil
— sheet glass or metal
— foil-backed plasterboard (known as insulating plasterboard)
— 'vapour check' plasterboard (polythene backed)
— enamelled hardboard
— gloss paint on dense plaster
— glazed tiles with waterproof joints
— vinyl wallpaper on dense plaster.

Great care must be taken to ensure that all joints are sealed and there are no holes in the vapour check (fig 9).
Anti-condensation emulsion paint (eg Silexine 'Anticon') is useful in 'marginal' conditions: it will stop condensation dripping from a cold water pipe in a heated room, and prevent mould growth. However, it is not a vapour barrier and so condensation can form under it, for example, if it is applied to a solid brick external wall. It does not provide a long term solution.
Further information is given in the DoE Booklets 'Condensation in dwellings'.

fig. 9   detail cross-section

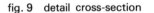

— existing wall
— insulation
— vapour check
— internal lining board
— batten

fig. 10

gully

fig. 11

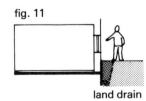

land drain

fig. 12

rain

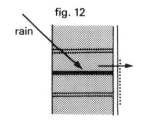

3 PENETRATION OF RAIN AND MOISTURE FROM OUTSIDE
The first step is gardening, as in Section 1, where the external ground level is higher than internal floor level. A drainage channel should be provided outside and the ground terraced down, or held up by a retaining wall (fig 10).
Alternatively, a trench should be dug and the outside wall-face given a waterproof-render or bitumen coating. The trench can then be backfilled. A land drain can be incorporated (fig 11).
Solid walls are more liable to damp penetration than cavity walls, particularly if the joints are defective. 'Falling-damp' striking the top of a dpc may, in some circumstances, produce the effect of rising damp inside the house (fig 12).
Leaking gutters, roofs, rainwater pipes, flashings and wall joints should be repaired. Gaps around window and door frames should be sealed. Waterproof rendering or paint should not be applied unless the wall is insulated and has a vapour check, a dpc and no sign of 'efflorescence' on the outside (white salts on the surface). Even so, hairline cracks could form in the rendering, which let in the water; condensation can form behind the rendering and force it off the wall. A normal semi-porous rendering will provide protection from rain.
In the case of a solid wall, a waterproof lining and cavity on the inside is an effective solution (eg 'Newtonite' bituminous corrugated lining fixed with non-corrodible fastenings). Silicone-based waterproofers applied to the outside face will permit water vapour to pass through to the outside but require re-application every 2 or 3 years.

4 BUILT-IN MOISTURE

This is not found in an old house but will occur if 'wet trades' are involved in the improvement work, eg brickwork, concrete, plaster. Great care has to be taken, since the existing structure may be very dry and will therefore absorb any surplus water brought into the house: timber will swell if its moisture content increases.

An indication of the amounts of water which are built-in by the 'wet trades', is shown by the following:

10 m² (100 sq ft) of 100 mm (4 in) thick concrete slab contains 100 litres (22 gallons) of water.

10 m² (100 sq ft) of 13 mm ($\frac{1}{2}$ in) thick plaster contains 50 litres (11 gallons) of water.

Ventilation is essential to allow this water to evaporate to the atmosphere.

DAMPNESS IN TIMBER

The presence of moisture especially in unventilated spaces represents a danger to timber: these conditions might occur in roof spaces, cellars, behind skirting boards and frames, under timber floors and in painted external frames. Wherever there is moisture which cannot escape, and timber reaches a moisture content of more than 20 per cent, wet rot or dry rot may occur.

Wet rot (Cellar fungus). This is common in situations where severe wetting is encountered. Timber which is dried to below 20 per cent will remain immune from its attack and any existing decay will become inactive.

The fungus does not penetrate dry brickwork or plaster and is relatively easy to control by removing the source of moisture.

Treatment: The source of moisture must be located and eliminated and steps taken to dry out any residual moisture. Where members are structurally weakened these must be replaced or adequately supported. Where drying cannot be achieved, or may be delayed, existing timbers and replacement timbers should be treated with a preservative.

Dry rot. This is the most serious form of decay and is most common in situations of persistent dampness. As with wet rots a moisture content in excess of 20 per cent is necessary for its initiation but the subsequent growth can rapidly spread to surrounding dry timbers. This fungus can penetrate dry brickwork, plaster, etc, to reach apparently isolated timbers and a most careful examination is necessary to establish the full extent of an outbreak.

Treatment: The full extent of the attack must be determined and fully exposed. All visibly affected timber, and apparently sound timber 600 mm beyond, should be removed and burnt. Brickwork or plaster within 1 m of the outbreak should be sterilised with a masonry fungicide and in the case of thick walls the fluid should be irrigated by means of holes drilled at a downward angle at approximately 200 mm vertical and horizontal centres. Remaining sound timbers in the area should be liberally brush coated with a fungicide and replacement members pretreated by pressure impregnation with a preservative.

Where doubt as to the particular form of attack exists, expert advice should be sought.

Thermal insulation

Improved thermal insulation in existing houses will result in greater comfort and/or a reduction in the amount of heating fuel used. It seems likely that all fuels will continue to rise in price. A good standard of insulation also helps to solve condensation problems. Many insulation materials are relatively cheap and easy to install, and so 'do-it-yourself' labour can be used to keep installation costs down.

EXTERNAL WALLS

Solid brickwork, usually 225 mm or 38 mm (9 in or 13½ in) thick, or stone was used in most houses built before the 1920's. Cavity construction brickwork has been used since then, and it can be recognised externally usually by the 'stretcher-bond' pattern and by its overall thickness 260 mm to 290 mm (10½ in to 11½ in) including plaster on the inner face (fig 1).

The amount of heat loss per unit area (the 'U' value) through solid brickwork is high: in other words it is a poor insulator. The 'U' value of 225 mm brickwork is 2.67 w/m² °C (0.47 btu/ft² °F).

Cavity brickwork plastered on the inside has less heat loss: 'U' value 1.70 (0.30). The Building Regulations 1976 permit maximum 'U' values of 1.0 (0.18) for an external wall and a mean of 1.8 for the whole wall including glazed areas (taking a 'U' value for single glazing of 5.7, double glazing 2.8). This applies to new work, such as an extension.

Area × 'U' value × temperature differential = heat loss per hour

Example:
An extension 2 m wide, projecting 3 m from house, three external walls each 3 m high.

Total external wall area = 24 m² including single glazed window 1.2 m² and single glazed door 1.8 m².

Total glazed area 3 m² × 5.7 watts per m² per °C ('U' value)
= 17.1 watts per °C

Area of wall = 24−3 = 21 m² × 1.0 = 21+

38.1

38.1 ÷ 24 = 1.6

Perimeter wall average must not exceed 1.8

∴ 1.6 is acceptable

If the inner leaf of the cavity wall was built of lightweight concrete blocks in place of bricks or heavy concrete blocks, the insulation is considerably improved: 'U' value 0.96 (0.17). This construction is not found in houses more than about 20 years old.

Cavity injection

The insulation of older cavity walls can be greatly improved by injecting plastics foam (urea formaldehyde), polyurethane granules, or mineral-wool fibres into the cavity. This process is done by specialists, drilling holes from outside and pumping the material in under pressure. The 'U' value for 275 mm cavity brickwork with foam or fibre cavity-fill is 0.50 (0.09), which is a reduction of about two-thirds in the heat loss through the cavity wall.

There is a risk with walls exposed to driving rain, of moisture running across the metal wall-ties or mortar droppings in the filled cavity, and so into the house. The manufacturers claim that proper application will prevent this.

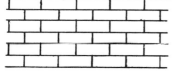

fig. 1 elevation

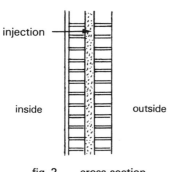

injection

inside   outside

fig. 2   cross-section

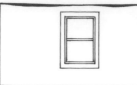

Fig. 3
Cross section

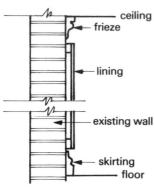

Fig. 4 Detail
cross section

(labels: ceiling, frieze, lining, existing wall, skirting, floor)

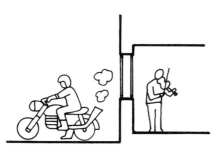

fig. 5

fig. 6

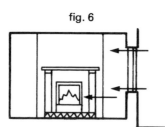

Improving solid walls

Cavity injection is impossible with solid walls, and so more expensive methods must be employed, either external cladding or internal lining. Internal lining has the disadvantage of reducing room dimensions and requiring light switches, wall sockets etc, to be repositioned. External cladding is more expensive still, and changes the external appearance.

It is easier and cheaper to adopt the 'projecting panel' principle (See fig 4) which requires no awkward cutting at top and bottom, and does not interfere with floor coverings, skirtings (and sockets fixed to the skirtings) or frieze mouldings: the 'character' of a room can therefore be kept. Additional advantages are the ease with which cables can be run along the top or bottom of the panel and the reduced possibility of rising damp attacking the lining.

There is always a danger with solid walls of moisture from rain penetrating to the inside and it is advisable to use treated battens and waterproof building paper (refer to the **chapter** 'Dealing with dampness').

Typical 'U' values:

1 225 mm (9 in) brickwork, plastered inner face 2.67 (0.47)

2 As 1, with 25 mm battens and 12.7 mm foil backed plasterboard 1.8 (0.32)

3 As 1, with 25 mm battens and 12.7 mm fibre insulation board 1.9 (0.34)

4 As 1, with 25 mm battens and 12.7 mm plasterboard with 25 mm glass fibre quilt between battens 0.8 (0.14)

It is essential when relying on the airspace as an insulator as in 2 and 3, to ensure that it is properly sealed against vapour from inside the building.

No account is taken in these 'U' values of openings such as doors and windows.

A vapour check should be provided on the 'warm' side of the insulation material (refer to the **chapter** 'Dealing with dampness').

WINDOWS

The heat loss through single glazing is very high:
'U' value of window in sheltered south facing position 3.97 (0.70)
'U' value of window in exposed north facing position 7.38 (1.30)
Double glazing with a 6 mm ($\frac{1}{4}$ in) gap between the panes of glass is considerably better than single glazing:
'U' value of double glazed window in sheltered south facing position 2.67 (0.47)
'U' value of double glazed window in exposed north facing position 3.80 (0.67)

However 2.67 in the best situation is no better than the 'U' value of 225 mm solid brickwork: Double-glazing is really a poor insulator, and no better than heavy curtains drawn across single glazing. The window area in old houses is usually small in proportion to the external wall area (less than 15%) and so putting in double glazing will have little effect on the heating bill, although its effect will be noticeable in reducing condensation and increasing comfort.

It is more advantageous to install double glazing where the windows are large, and particularly where sound insulation is required to reduce traffic noise etc (fig 5), in which case the gap should be at least 100 mm (4 in) wide. There are several companies in this profitable field of separate frame inner-windows, advertising widely in the press. Their products are usually well-made from good materials and are therefore expensive A similar reduction in heat loss can be achieved by sealing all draughts in the existing window.

Double glazing has the advantage, however, of reducing condensation on the window and down-draughts, which certainly improves the 'comfort' effect.

WEATHER STRIPPING

Elimination of draughts results in the most improvement for the least cost; gaps around windows and doors (fig 6) should be sealed, (there are several types of strip available). These gaps produce on average $1\frac{1}{2}$ air changes per hour (ie the volume of each room × $1\frac{1}{2}$) although $\frac{1}{2}$ to $\frac{3}{4}$ is adequate in most rooms. This amount can be provided by one small vent per room, with all other gaps sealed. Chimney flues should be sealed off with a panel whenever the hearth is not in use. The panel should have small vent-holes in it. Under floor air supply from the

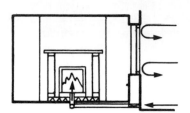

fig. 7

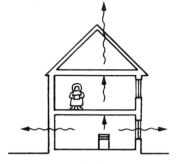

fig. 8

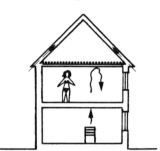

fig. 9

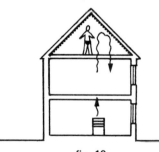

fig. 10

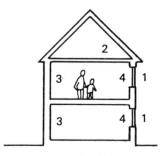

fig. 11

outside to a boiler or open fire is recommended to prevent draughts, and fewer air changes will result if a throat-restrictor is fitted at the bottom of the chimney (fig 7).

External doors should not be left open in winter, and a draught lobby into the house is recommended. Reduced ventilation may result in more condensation (refer to the chapter 'Dealing with dampness').

ROOF INSULATION is the next step to be taken. In terrace houses the roof area is sometimes as much as the external wall areas. Old houses usually had tiles or slates on battens fixed direct to the rafters: ventilation of the roof space was excellent (a gap between each tile) which prevented rot forming, but also permitted heat from the house to escape straight through the roof (fig 8). It is sometimes necessary to replace old battens and/or rafters due to insect attack. The tiles or slates should be stripped off (they can be re-used) and the battens removed, so that tiling-felt can be fixed over the rafters. New battens are then fixed and the tiles or slates replaced. The effect of the tiling-felt is to create a windless cavity in the roof which acts to some extent as an insulator. Permanent ventilation is required at the eaves to discourage rot in the roof timbers. Insulation is best provided at ceiling level by: (fig 9)

— laying quilt (glass-fibre or mineral-wool) over the joists,
or
— spreading granular material between the joists (eg gypsum, vermiculite, cork, polystyrene),
or
— fixing a new ceiling.

If the roof is to be used as habitable space, then the insulation should be fixed to the rafters: (fig 10)

— by laying quilt over the rafters (before laying the tiling-felt. A polythene vapour check layer should be laid under the quilt
or
— by fixing fibre insulating board, foil backed plasterboard or other sheet materials to the underside of the rafters, with quilt between the rafters.

The Building Regulations 1976 require new house roofs to have a 'U' value of not more than 0.60 (0.11).

Old roofs with tiles on battens and a plaster ceiling have a very poor 'U' value; approximately 3.00 (0.56). Addition of tiling felt will improve this to approximately 2.00 (0.35).

25 mm (1 in) glass-fibre or mineral-wool quilt laid over the ceiling joists gives a 'U' value of 0.73 (0.128) (0.84 if laid between joists). To comply with the Building Regulations 1976 a 50 mm (2 in) glass-fibre or mineral-wool quilt laid over the ceiling joists is needed; 'U' value 0.49 (0.086) (0.54 if laid between joists). The thickness of expanded vermiculite granules required between the joists to achieve the same results are 40 mm and 80 mm.

SUMMARY

The order of carrying out insulation improvements to achieve greatest effect from the start with the least cost is as follows:

1 WEATHER STRIPPING of doors and windows.
2 ROOF INSULATION.
3 WALL INSULATION.
4 DOUBLE GLAZING.

It may be worthwhile considering dry lining or double glazing an exposed north wall or in a living room only.

DoE have produced a publication 'Warmth kept in' which discusses insulation. Houses which are being improved with the help of local authority improvement or intermediate grants have to comply with the current Building Regulations Part F Roof Insulation.

A survey carried out by Applied Research of Cambridge Ltd, and the Cambridge School of Architecture, compares the cost of these methods with the estimated savings in heating bills. The figures shown are for a two-storey semi-detached house, floor area 100 m², (2 floors x 50 m²), roof area 50 m², external wall area 100 m², window area 20 m², with brick cavity walls, uninsulated roof space and single glazing. (Values for other houses will vary according to the amount of external wall, windows, roof area etc. A terrace house has less heat loss than a detached or semi-detached house of the same size due to the small amount of external wall involved).

	Cost	% heating bill saving
1 Weather stripping to reduce air changes from $1\frac{1}{2}$ to 1 per hour	£5	6%
2 Roof insulation 50 mm (2 in) glass-fibre quilt	£20	8%
3 Walls. Injected foam cavity infill	£75	18%
4 Double glazing all windows	£200	10%
TOTAL	£300	42%

Annual heating bill £150.   42 per cent saving = £63.

The cost of insulation will be saved in **5 years,** or less if fuel prices continue to rise.

Note:

Items 1 + 2 + 3 = £100 cost, giving 32 per cent fuel saving together.
Item   4 = £200 cost, giving 10 per cent fuel saving.

Greater savings are possible but greater capital investment is required:

	Cost	% heating bill saving
1 Weather stripping from $1\frac{1}{2}$ to $\frac{1}{2}$ air-change/hour	£10	12%
2 Roof 100 m quilt (4 in)	£40	12%
3 Walls. Injected foam and dry lining	£500	27%
4 Double glazing	£200	10%
TOTAL	£750	61%

Dry-lining may be necessary for reasons other than insulation (eg dilapidated condition of wall surfaces.

An important additional factor in insulation is that a well insulated surface does not attract dirt as quickly as an uninsulated surface, so decoration costs will be reduced over the years.

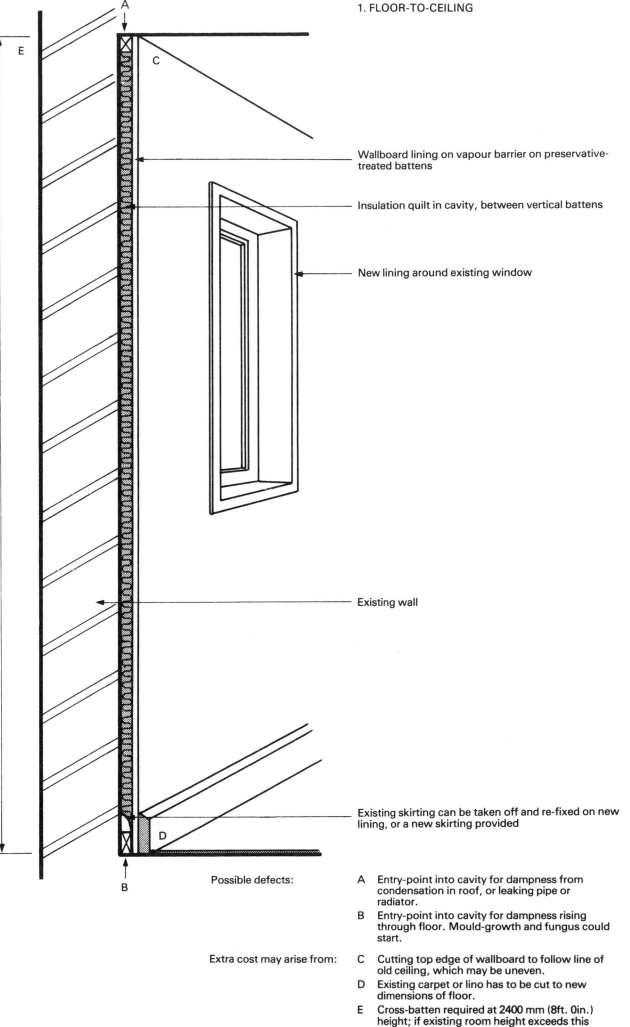

1. FLOOR-TO-CEILING

Wallboard lining on vapour barrier on preservative-treated battens

Insulation quilt in cavity, between vertical battens

New lining around existing window

Existing wall

Existing skirting can be taken off and re-fixed on new lining, or a new skirting provided

Existing room height = wall lining height

Possible defects:

A   Entry-point into cavity for dampness from condensation in roof, or leaking pipe or radiator.

B   Entry-point into cavity for dampness rising through floor. Mould-growth and fungus could start.

Extra cost may arise from:

C   Cutting top edge of wallboard to follow line of old ceiling, which may be uneven.

D   Existing carpet or lino has to be cut to new dimensions of floor.

E   Cross-batten required at 2400 mm (8ft. 0in.) height; if existing room height exceeds this (sheet-size).

15

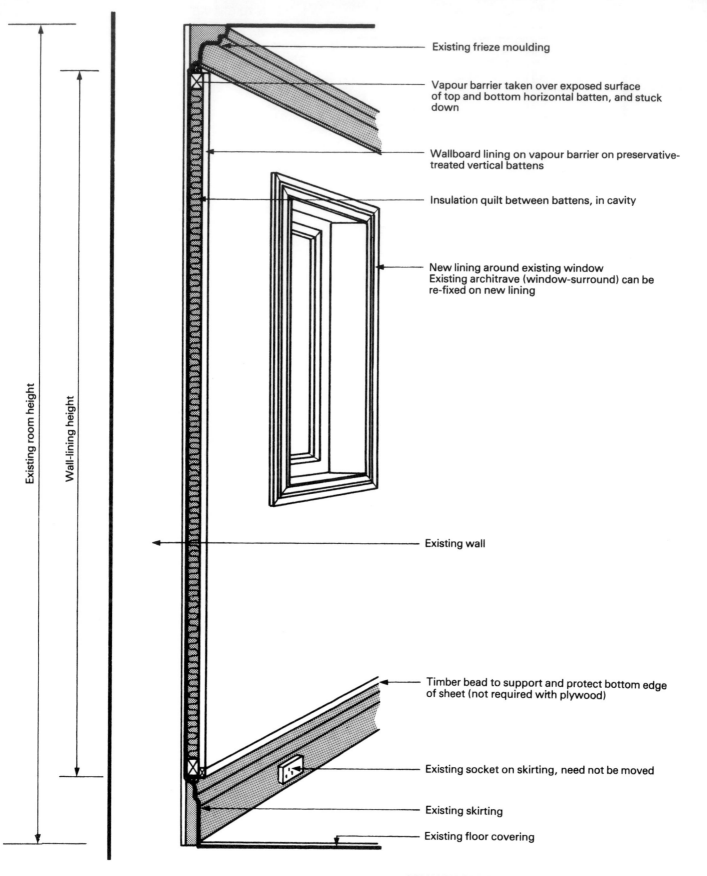

Existing frieze moulding

Vapour barrier taken over exposed surface of top and bottom horizontal batten, and stuck down

Wallboard lining on vapour barrier on preservative-treated vertical battens

Insulation quilt between battens, in cavity

New lining around existing window
Existing architrave (window-surround) can be re-fixed on new lining

Existing wall

Timber bead to support and protect bottom edge of sheet (not required with plywood)

Existing socket on skirting, need not be moved

Existing skirting

Existing floor covering

Existing room height

Wall-lining height

ADVANTAGES OVER METHOD 1

Appearance: 'Character' of old house retained, especially if attractive frieze and skirting mouldings exist. Floor and ceiling sizes not altered.

Convenience: Cables can run along top or bottom.

Durability: Dampness cannot enter from floor or ceiling.

Cost: Less wallboard and vertical battens length. No awkward cutting at ceiling. No cutting of existing carpet or lino.

16

Sound insulation

Under Part G of the Building Regulations certain walls and floors are required to provide adequate resistance to the transmission of sound. This applies to 'new work' only.

WALLS
Regulation G1 (1)
The walls listed below must adequately resist the transmission of airborne sound, in conjunction with the associated construction:
— separating wall between PG I houses in a terrace or semi-detached
— separating wall between a PG I house and another building
— separating wall between a habitable room in a flat (or maisonette) and any other part of the building not used exclusively with that flat (or maisonette).

Regulation G1 (2) & (3)
The wall between a refuse chute and a habitable room must have a mass of not less than 1320 kg/m² (270 lb/ft²) whereas a wall between a refuse chute and any part of a dwelling except a habitable room must be not less than 220 kg/m² (45 lb/ft²), unless they are of cavity construction and the leaves are independent of each other.

Regulation G2 (2)
Schedule 12 Part 1 lists the 'deemed to satisfy' constructions. These include:
— a solid wall not less than 415 kg/m² (85 lb/ft²) including plaster
or
— a wall with a cavity not less than 50 mm and a mass not less than 415 kg/m² including plaster
or
— a wall with a cavity not less than 75 mm and a mass not less than 250 kg/m² (51 lb/ft²) including plaster.
Additionally, the 'deemed to satisfy' construction is required to:
— Extend at least 460 mm (18 in) beyond an external flanking wall
or
— be tied or bonded into one leaf of an external flanking wall which is not less than 120 kg/m² and in which any opening is not less than 690 mm (27 in) from the opposite side of the separating wall (unless the opening height is not more than $\frac{2}{3}$ storey height and the external flanking wall above and below the opening extends not less than 3 m on both sides of the separating wall)
or
— extend to the outer face of an external flanking wall of timber or other light construction and at top and bottom is tied or bonded to a solid ground floor or suspended concrete floor not less than 220 kg/m² or a concrete roof not less than 145 kg/m².

Note that these constructions may give unsatisfactory sound insulation if lightweight plaster or plasterboard on plaster dabs is applied, instead of traditional plaster unless the brick or blockwork of the separating wall initially is rendered with sand based cement. The modern practice of economising on mortar by laying bricks 'frogs down' and with open 'perpends' is also unsatisfactory.

Regulation G2 (1)
Permits other wall constructions provided they satisfy the required insulation values at 16 frequencies as shown on the graph:
23 dB total adverse deviation below these values is permitted.

AIRBORNE SOUND INSULATION

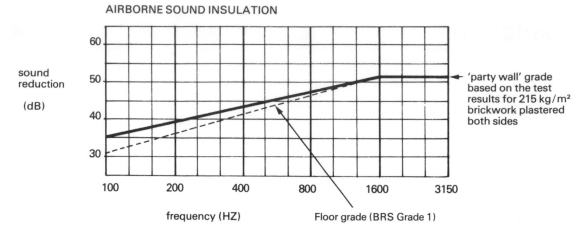

sound reduction (dB)

frequency (HZ)

'party wall' grade based on the test results for 215 kg/m² brickwork plastered both sides

Floor grade (BRS Grade 1)

TRADA has tested timber frame constructions which satisfy this grade: eg Watery Lane 4-storey maisonettes, High Wycombe, has loadbearing party walls:

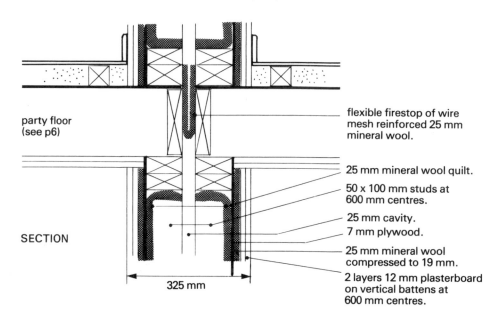

party floor (see p6)

SECTION

325 mm

flexible firestop of wire mesh reinforced 25 mm mineral wool.

25 mm mineral wool quilt.

50 x 100 mm studs at 600 mm centres.

25 mm cavity.

7 mm plywood.

25 mm mineral wool compressed to 19 mm.

2 layers 12 mm plasterboard on vertical battens at 600 mm centres.

Sound insulation, tested in situ, is below the grade at the 4 lowest frequencies but better than the grade at upper frequencies. The total adverse deviation is 14 dB. This construction gives 1 hour fire resistance under fully loaded conditions. It proves conclusively that separate framed partitions can provide sound insulation as effectively as solid heavy construction.

IMPROVEMENTS TO EXISTING WALLS

Although Part G does not apply to the 'existing', it is highly desirable to reduce sound transmission as much as possible: modern life is noisy (radio, TV, hi-fi, washing machine, vacuum cleaner, spindryer, etc).
A common source of sound transmission between houses in a terrace or semi-detached, is via the roofspace:
If there is no separating wall in the roof space then one should be built. Usually, there is a separating wall but it is unplastered and has defective mortar joints. The wall should be rendered with two coats sand/cement to seal all air gaps.
External sound transmission can occur through adjacent windows:
This can be remedied by:
a Extending the separating wall outside or
b Repositioning the window or
c Adding an inner window with an air gap of at least 100 mm, and sound absorption material around the air gap.

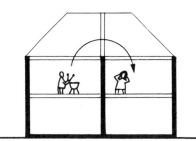

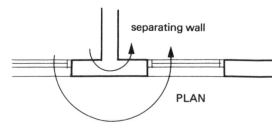

separating wall

PLAN

Constructing an 'innerleaf' stud partition can considerably reduce sound transmission, although the room width will be reduced by approximately 120 mm.

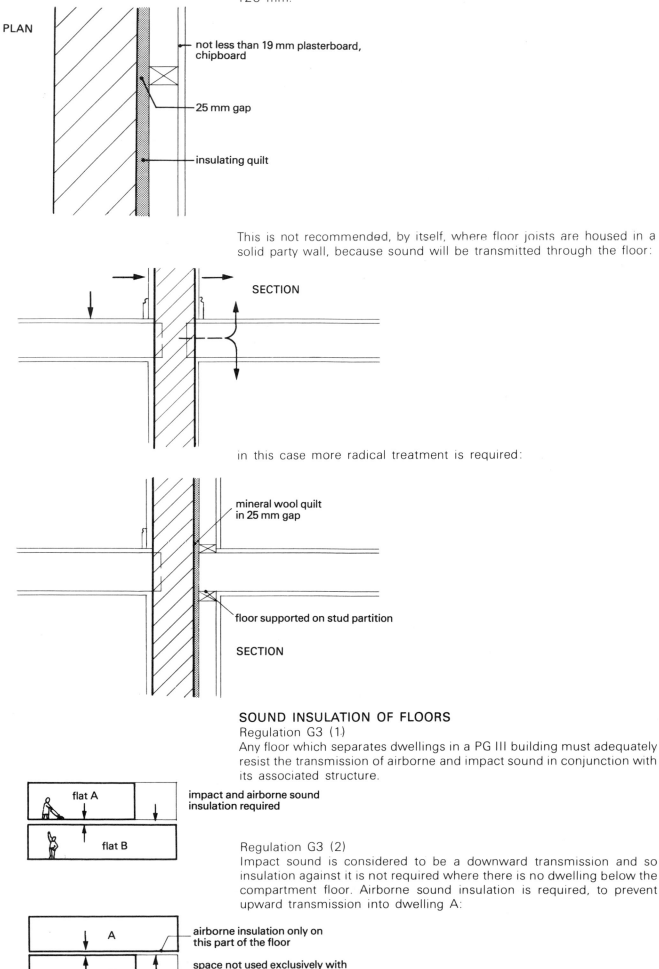

PLAN

not less than 19 mm plasterboard, chipboard

25 mm gap

insulating quilt

This is not recommended, by itself, where floor joists are housed in a solid party wall, because sound will be transmitted through the floor:

SECTION

in this case more radical treatment is required:

mineral wool quilt in 25 mm gap

floor supported on stud partition

SECTION

SOUND INSULATION OF FLOORS
Regulation G3 (1)
Any floor which separates dwellings in a PG III building must adequately resist the transmission of airborne and impact sound in conjunction with its associated structure.

flat A

flat B

impact and airborne sound insulation required

Regulation G3 (2)
Impact sound is considered to be a downward transmission and so insulation against it is not required where there is no dwelling below the compartment floor. Airborne sound insulation is required, to prevent upward transmission into dwelling A:

A

B

airborne insulation only on this part of the floor

space not used exclusively with dwelling A, or machinery or tank room

The intermediate floor in a maisonette is not a compartment floor, and so no sound insulation is required.

The required standard of sound insulation for compartment floors in the case of 'new work' is shown on the graph, page 18. Schedule 12 Part 2 in the Building Regulations, lists the 'deemed to satisfy' constructions: these include heavy concrete floors not less than 220 kg/m² with 'floating' floor finishes, and one timber construction.

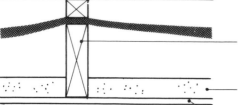

boarding nailed to battens laid on quilt — *not nailed to joists*

floor joist

pugging

lath and plaster or plasterboard (not less than 19 mm)

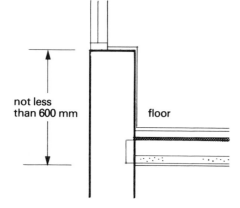

not less than 600 mm

floor

'Deemed to satisfy' timber floor: impact and airborne sound insulation provided that
— Combined mass of ceiling and pugging is not less than 120 kg/m² (eg 50 mm sand + 19 mm plasterboard)
— the floor is bounded below on at least 3 sides by walls with average mass 415 kg/m² (equivalent to 215 mm (9 in) brickwork)
— any opening in an external flanking wall does not occur within 600 mm above the soffit of the floor, unless the floor projects to form a balcony.

SECTIONS

balcony

The quilt should be turned up around the perimeter to isolate the floorboards.

This construction is unsatisfactory in 'new work' due to:
a The practical problem of fixing the ceiling and the pugging before the floorboards (the reverse of normal procedure)
b possible staining of the ceiling by sand
c problem of fixing light fittings, due to sand
d 'floating' floors are 'spongy' to walk on; this could be omitted however, if the floor is required to provide airborne sound insulation only.

Regulation G4 (1)
Permits alternative constructions which satisfy Grade 1 when tested.
A total adverse deviation of 23 dB measured at the 16 frequencies is permitted. (See graph on p18).

TRADA has installed compartment floors in 4-storey PG III buildings at: Watery Lane, High Wycombe which satisfy Building Regulations requirements (impact & airborne) in conjunction with timber frame walls (see detail on p 18).

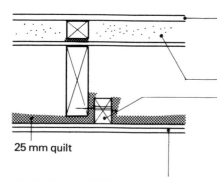

12.7 mm plywood on polythene sheet on 50 x 50 mm battens on resilient pads on polythene sheet on 6 mm plywood

sand pugging between battens

ceiling supported from joists by resilient mounting (battens nailed through rubber sleeves, or ceiling fixed by 'Gyproc' resilient bars)

25 mm quilt

double layer of 12.7 mm plasterboard

(The polythene sheet is to prevent sand falling through the joints or being sucked up through the joints by a vacuum cleaner)

This construction has several advantages over the 'deemed to satisfy' floor:

a the ceilings are fixed after the floors
b the sand cannot stain the ceiling
c the floor is not 'spongy' to walk on.
d no problems of salt cellar effect at electric ceiling fittings.

EXISTING FLOORS

Part G does not apply to existing floors which become compartment floors when the building is converted from PG I to PG III. Nevertheless, the occupants of flats or maisonettes will regard the sound insulation of such floors as highly desirable; for this reason TRADA has carried out a series of acoustic tests on different methods of upgrading the sound insulation of existing floors. The results are summarised as follows:

1 Existing floors in old houses tend to have thick floorboards and thick lath and plaster ceilings, with better sound insulation than modern 'non-compartment' floors. They should be kept where possible.

2 All air gaps should be sealed, particularly those between plain-edged floorboards: hardboard pinned down on the boards will reduce direct sound transmission considerably. 'Tempered hardboard' should be used as a floor finish, but if it is to be covered with carpet or tiles etc, then standard hardboard is cheaper. If $\frac{1}{2}$ hour fire resistance is required then the hardboard should have a minimum thickness of 5 mm if the ceiling is thick plaster and lath.

3 Adding to the mass of the ceiling will improve sound insulation (eg a layer of 9.5 mm plasterboard).

4 The 'deemed to satisfy' construction for new timber floors (see p 4) is unsuitable for improving existing timber floors, for the following reasons:

a The existing joists probably cannot support the extra weight of sand pugging (not less then 80 kg/m²), and the existing ceiling below the joists might collapse under the weight anyway.

b 'Floating' the floorboards on old joists will almost certainly produce rocking unless the joist tops are levelled off.

c Raising the floor level by using the 'floating floor' construction will create problems with existing doors, skirtings and stair heights particularly: adding say 50 mm onto the height of the top riser will make the stair very dangerous to walk down, and will not be permitted. All risers must be equal in a stair and so it is necessary to add increasingly **thicker amounts to each tread in order to achieve equal risers, or, to leave the floor of the 'landing' untouched — stopping the floating floor treatment at each doorway onto the loading.**

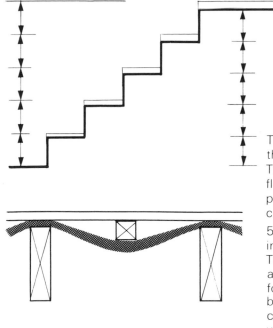

The extra height can be reduced by laying the floorboards directly onto the quilt:
The battens are still required (between the joists) in order to hold the floorboards together. This requires some prefabrication of flooring panels; the battens should project at either side so that adjacent panels can be screwed together.

5 TRADA's recommended method is to add a second ceiling supported independently of the floor above it.
This has several advantages:
a Many old houses have ceiling heights which are probably excessive for the rooms in a modern flat (particularly if a large room is subdivided).
b The existing ceiling may be in need of repair and decoration.
c The remedial work is carried out entirely in the room below the floor, where the improved sound insulation is required, unlike the 'deemed to satisfy' construction which is constructed from above the floor.
The new ceiling should be airtight and weigh not less than 25 kg/m² (eg one layer of 19 mm plasterboard plus ceiling joists and 25 mm quilt). There should be at least 25 mm clearance between the existing ceiling and the top of the new joists. The limiting factor will probably be the 2300 mm headroom required in a habitable room below the ceiling.

The new ceiling joists at 600 mm centres should span the shortest dimension of the room, for economy, and will therefore usually be parallel to the existing floor joists.

The ceiling joists are supported at each end on a 50 x 38 mm ledger batten plugged and screwed to the wall. The joists are notched over the ledger — provided the joist depth is not less than 100 mm. (See detail p 24).

The plasterboard ceiling should extend under the ledger, for fire resistance and sound insulation purposes.

Sound insulation tests were carried out at the Building Research Station with 18 variations of the separate-ceiling theme.

The test floor measured 4560 x 3650 mm (14 ft 11½ in x 12 ft 0 in), with 50 x 175 mm floor joists at 375 mm centres (2 x 7 in at 15 in centres). The 50 x 100 mm ceiling joists were installed at 600 mm centres (2 x 4 in at 24 in centres). The cavity between new and old ceilings was

125 mm (5 in) in tests 4, 7 and 9.
250 mm (10 in) in tests 5 and 10.
375 mm (15 in) in tests 6, 8 and 11.

None of the airborne sound insulation results came within the permitted total 23 dB adverse deviation from Grade 1 (test 5 was best with 37 dB adverse deviation). However, 10 results satisfied Grade 2 — floors 5, 10, 9, 6, 4, 11, 8, 14, 7, 13.

Seven of the test results came within the permitted 23 dB adverse deviation from Grade 1 impact sound insulation (floors 9, 5, 11, 10, 13, 6, 14) and a further 8 satisfied Grade 2 adverse deviation (floors 4, 8, 7, 12, 17, 15, 16, 3).

Some of the airborne results (including those tests with 375 mm cavities) were adversely affected by flanking transmission down the perimeter wall, which on 3 sides of the test chamber was the inner leaf of a cavity wall. Old houses with thick solid walls should have less flanking transmission and therefore produce better airborne sound insulation results.

The existing floor in the test chamber had 19 mm thick plain edge boarding and a 22 mm ceiling (9.5 + 12.5 mm plasterboard).

Adding a new ceiling of type No 4, 5, 6, 9, 10, 11, 13 or 14 will give airborne and impact sound insulation almost to Building Regulations deemed to satisfy standard — in conjunction with thick solid flanking walls.

The particular choice depends on the existing ceiling height: Building Regulation K8 'Height of habitable rooms' does not apply to the 'existing' when a house is converted into flats or maisonettes. However, the installation of a new self supporting ceiling and internal partitions etc counts as 'new work'. It is desirable therefore to provide not less than 2300 mm (7 ft 6½ in) ceiling height in habitable rooms. This will determine the airspace depth of the new ceiling. The following table indicates which ceiling type is suitable:

Existing ceiling height	Proposed ceiling height	Use ceiling No
(8 ft 10½ in) 2700 mm & over	2300 mm (7 ft 6½ in)	6 or 11
(8 ft 4½ in) 2550 to 2700 mm	2300 mm	5 or 10
(8 ft 0 in) 2440 to 2550 mm	2300 mm	4 or 9*
(7 ft 8 in) 2340 to 2440 mm	2300 mm	13 or 14

*Note the limitations on joist-span with these 2 ceilings (see p24).

Generally, the tests showed that a heavy ceiling with a small airspace is as effective as a lighter ceiling with a larger airspace. Therefore, if ceiling height is not critical, the cheapest of the most effective ceilings can be used:

in test 5 the airspace was 250 mm

in test 6 the airspace was 375 mm

(weight of new construction 25 kg/m²)

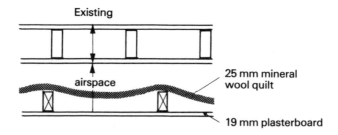

Existing

airspace

25 mm mineral wool quilt

19 mm plasterboard

Where the existing ceiling height is insufficient for the use of types 5 or 6 then the same construction can be used with an airspace of 125 mm (test 4). This will be less effective than 5 or 6, however. Test 9 gave very good results, but is more expensive than 4 due to the addition of a second layer to the ceiling:

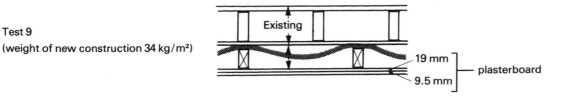

Test 9
(weight of new construction 34 kg/m²)

19 mm
9.5 mm } — plasterboard

Tests 10 and 11 were of the same heavier construction, with airspaces of 250 and 375 mm respectively. Either of these will probably give the best results of all the alternative types, in conjunction with thick solid flanking walls.
The tests proved the effectiveness of having mineral-wool quilt in the airspace: it reduces the reflection of soundwaves between the new and old ceilings and between the new joists.
Where the existing ceiling height is insufficient for the use of types 4 or 9 then 13 or 14 should be used. The existing ceiling has to be removed and a heavy ceiling added with new ceiling joists running along between the floor joists. 13 or 14 are therefore more expensive than any of the other ceilings described here, and gave worse results in the tests.

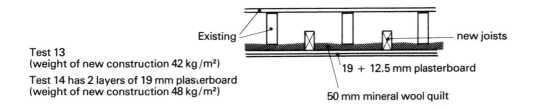

Existing — new joists
19 + 12.5 mm plasterboard
50 mm mineral wool quilt

Test 13
(weight of new construction 42 kg/m²)

Test 14 has 2 layers of 19 mm plasterboard
(weight of new construction 48 kg/m²)

The effectiveness of 13 or 14 can probably be improved by fixing the mineral-wool quilt to the underside of the existing floor, thus reducing reflected sound in the airspace:

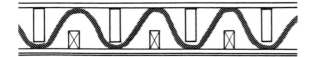

The ceiling joists in 13 or 14 have to be spaced according to the existing floor joists, which are usually about 350 to 500 mm apart (14 to 20 in), and so the more economical 600 mm spacing possible with the other ceiling types cannot be used. Maximum permitted spans for ceilings 13 and 14 are:

1 Joists at 350 mm centres:

a	b kg/m²	c=*b × 0.35 ÷ 5	Maximum spans mm d 50 x 100 mm joists	e 50 x 125 mm joists
13	42	2.94	3800	4700
14	48	3.36	3600	4500

2 Joists at 400 mm centres:

13	42	3.36	3600	4500
14	48	3.84	3450	4300

3 Joists at 450 mm centres:

13	42	3.78	3500	4300
14	48	4.32	3300	4200

4 Joists at 500 mm centres:

13	42	4.20	3350	4200
14	48	4.80	3200	4000

*(refer to p24 for notes on a b c d e and timber species used).

SOUND INSULATION OF EXISTING FLOORS
Joist sizes for new ceilings

a	b	c	d	e
			maximum span	
Detail No	Deadweight of ceiling including joists (kg/m²)*	Load carried per joist (kg/1 m run/ 1 cm width)	for 50 x 100 mm joist (mm)	maximum span for 50 x 125 mm (mm)
4	25	3	3750	
5	25	3	3750	4700
6	25	3	3750	4700
9	34	4.2	3400	
10	34	4.2	3400	4200
11	34	4.2	3400	4200
13	42	5.0	3200	4000
14	48	5.8	3000	3800

Ceiling joists at 600 mm centres, joist width 50 mm

The values in column c = the values in column b x 0.600 ÷ 5
= the values in column b x 0.12

The values in column c can be used directly on the appropriate timber species chart in the TRADA publication 'Span charts for solid timber beams' to find the maximum spans permitted with load sharing between joists.

Columns d and e show the spans for 100 mm and 125 mm deep joists in S2 group softwood or in redwood and whitewood species. (Air-dry timber).

The spans are limited by deflection (not more than 0.003 x span) and thus by the 'mean E' value, which is the same for S2 and redwood/whitewood. (0.83 N/cm² x 10⁶). The lowest stress grade can be used for any timber in these groups.

*No superimposed loads on the ceiling.

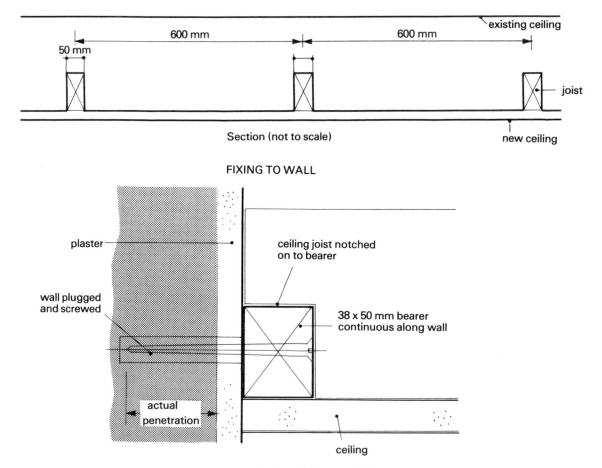

Section (not to scale)

FIXING TO WALL

Ceiling joists at 600 mm centres.

The load transmitted at each joist end = the ceiling deadweight (kg/m²) x area supported per joist end.

The heaviest load of the alternative ceilings in the table, is No 14 at 3800 mm span: the transmitted load = 48 x 3.8 x 0.3 = 60.8 kg.

From table 25 in CP 112 Part 2 : 1972, size 12 steel screws (5.6 mm diameter) at 600 mm centres will safely carry this load if the actual penetration is not less than 41 mm. Therefore, a 100 mm (4 in) long screw is suitable if the plaster is not more than 21 mm thick (41 + 21 + 38 = 100).

The wall should be drilled to take the appropriate fixing plug. If the wall is of suspect material (eg crumbling stone, clay lump, soft brick) it may be necessary to put the plugs and screws at closer centres, or to use expanding bolts.

In the case of ceilings lighter than that shown above, smaller gauge screws can be used (refer to CP 112 Part 2 : 1972), although the cost saving compared with the use of 100 mm No 12 screws will be minimal.

IMPROVEMENTS TO THE FLOOR SURFACE

Any of the alternatives described for improving sound insulation will be further improved by providing a resilient layer on top of the floorboards, eg carpet on underfelt, cork tiles, foam backed sheet flooring, rubber strip. A layer of fibre insulation board under hardboard under any of these finishes should give further improvement.

FIRE RESISTANCE

Any one of the separate ceilings described will contribute to the fire resistance of the floor (they do not enter the category of 'suspended ceilings' as in Regulation E6 'Fire resistance of floors in conjunction with suspended ceilings').

The 'deemed to satisfy' floor constructions for 1 hour, $\frac{1}{2}$ hour and modified $\frac{1}{2}$ hour fire resistance, together with alternative methods of improving existing floors are shown in 'Fire precautions' chapter. Adding a separate ceiling will increase the existing period of fire resistance provided by the floor.

A fire test was carried out as part of this project, using a construction similar to acoustic test No 13: 12.5 + 19 mm plasterboard ceiling under 48 x 75 mm joists at 300 mm centres running along between the 48 x 180 mm floor joists which supported 22 mm t and g floorboards. 50 mm mineral-wool quilt was laid over the ceiling.

This construction achieved over 1 hour fire resistance (86 mins actually) under fully loaded conditions. It is safe to say that reducing the quilt thickness to 25 mm will still achieve 1 hour.

Fire precautions

5

Regulation E5 requires 'elements of structure' to have fire-resistance for not less than the relevant periods specified (these vary with the type and size of building). This applies to 'new work' in the case of improvements to a PG I house ('no change of use') and where there is a 'change of use' from PG I to PG III. Regulation E15 applies to 'new work.'

Regulations are not retroactive and therefore do not apply to existing and unaltered work.

Note that 'new work' must not adversely affect the 'existing' in either case.

The 'elements of structure' are:

a any part of the structural frame except the roof

b any floor, including a compartment floor, except the lowest floor of a building ('a compartment floor' is a floor separating a flat or maisonette from another flat or maisonette or from any other part of the same building.* A PG I house has no compartment floors)

c an external wall

d a separating wall (ie party wall between adjoining buildings)‡

e a compartment wall (between flats or maisonettes)

f structure enclosing a protected shaft

g a loadbearing wall or loadbearing part of a wall

h a gallery (within a room)

PG I

a, b but not 'compartment floor', c, and g will occur in a PG I house which is completely detached. h could be included.

a, b but not 'compartment floor', c, d and g will occur in a PG I house which is semi-detached or in a terrace. h could be included.

PG III

a, b, c, e if there is more than dwelling per floor, f and g will occur in a PG III building which is completely detached. h could be included.

a, b, c, d, e if there is more than one dwelling per floor, f and g will occur in a PG III building which is semi-detached or in a terrace. h could be included.

*Note that the intermediate floor inside a maisonette is not a compartment floor.

‡each house in a terrace or semi-detached is considered as a building.

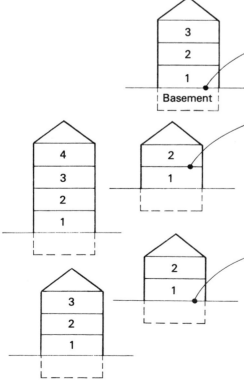

The required periods of fire resistance for the 'elements of structure' are:
for a PG I house – 'no change of use'

not exceeding 3-storeys   ½ hour

applies to 'new work' only

if there is a basement the area of which is 50 m² or more, the floor over it must have 1 hour fire resistance.

Note: 3-storeys is the limit for timber framed external walls within 1 m of the relevant boundary.

The 1st floor in a 2-storey PG I house can be modified ½ hour (ie 30 mins 'freedom from collapse' and 15 mins 'insulation' and 'resistance to passage of flame').

4-storeys   1 hour

except floors, which can be ½ hour (although any supporting beam, or any part of the floor which contributes to the structural support of the building, must be 1 hour).

PG I House converted to PG III use – 'change of use'

not exceeding 2-storeys   ½ hour

applies to 'new work' and to 'existing'

floor above basement 50 m² or larger must have 1 hour fire resistance and be made of non-combustible materials.

3-storeys   1 hour

non-compartment floors can be ½ hour (although any supporting beam, or any part of the floor which contributes to the structural support of the building, must be 1 hour).

Improved resistance to existing floors.

Examples taken from 'Deemed to Satisfy' Schedule 8 Part VII the Building Regulations 1976.

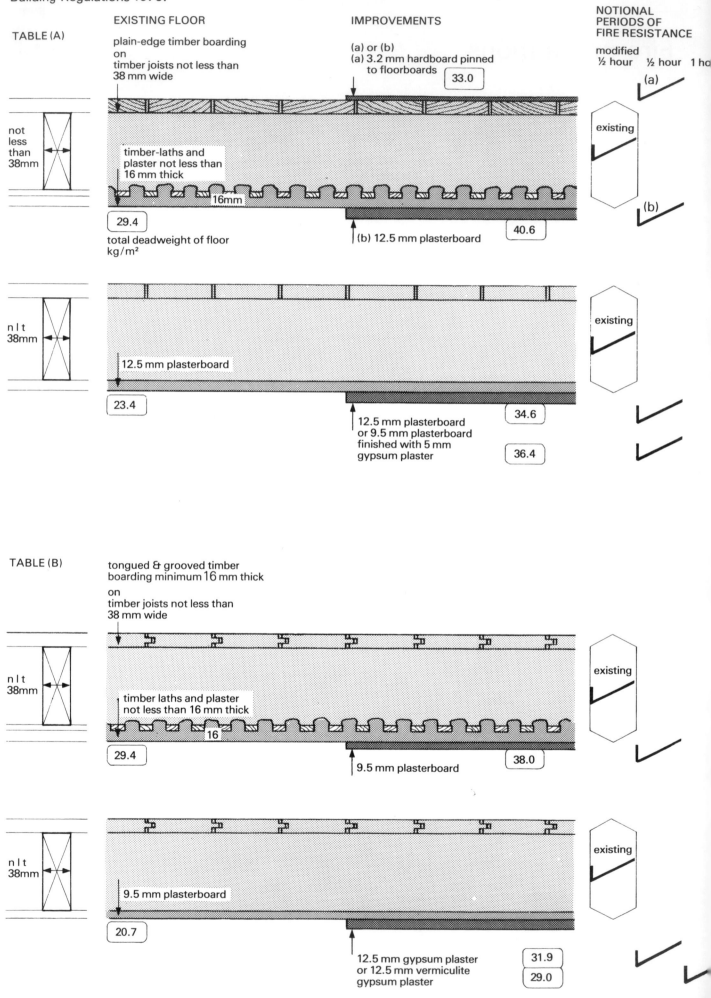

TABLE (A)

EXISTING FLOOR

plain-edge timber boarding
on
timber joists not less than 38 mm wide

not less than 38mm

timber-laths and plaster not less than 16 mm thick

16mm

29.4

total deadweight of floor kg/m²

IMPROVEMENTS

(a) or (b)
(a) 3.2 mm hardboard pinned to floorboards

33.0

(b) 12.5 mm plasterboard

40.6

NOTIONAL PERIODS OF FIRE RESISTANCE

modified
½ hour   ½ hour   1 ho

(a)

existing

(b)

n l t 38mm

12.5 mm plasterboard

23.4

existing

12.5 mm plasterboard or 9.5 mm plasterboard finished with 5 mm gypsum plaster

34.6

36.4

TABLE (B)

tongued & grooved timber boarding minimum 16 mm thick

on
timber joists not less than 38 mm wide

n l t 38mm

timber laths and plaster not less than 16 mm thick

16

29.4

existing

9.5 mm plasterboard

38.0

n l t 38mm

9.5 mm plasterboard

20.7

existing

12.5 mm gypsum plaster or 12.5 mm vermiculite gypsum plaster

31.9

29.0

28

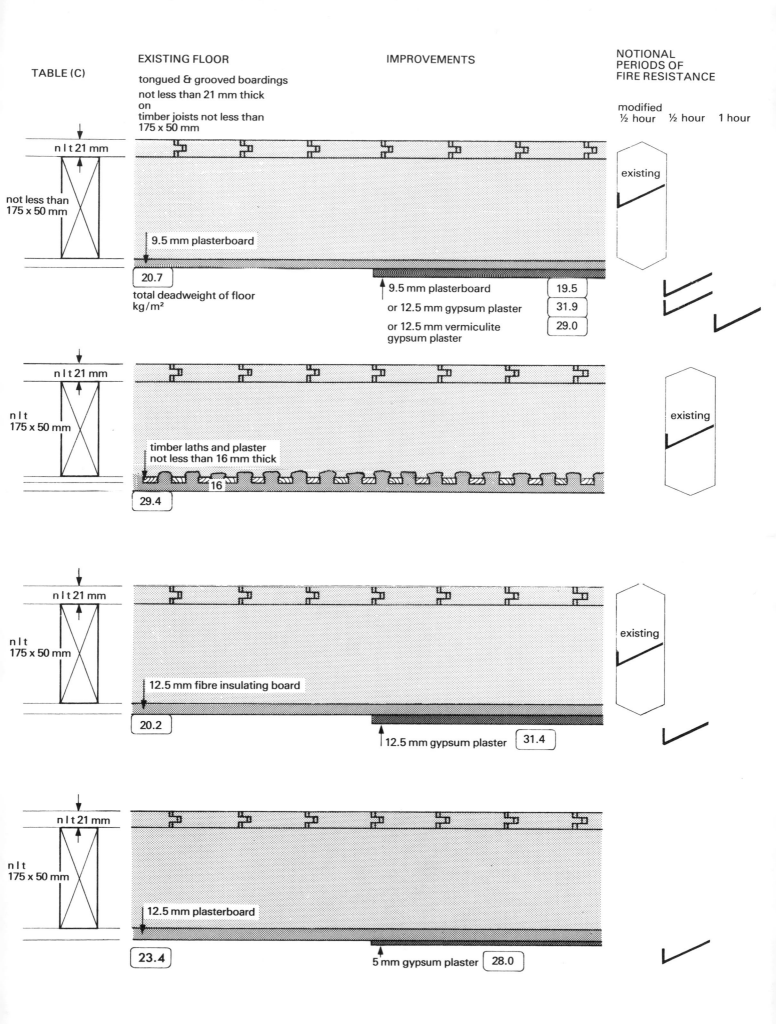

TABLE (C)

EXISTING FLOOR

tongued & grooved boardings
not less than 21 mm thick
on
timber joists not less than
175 x 50 mm

IMPROVEMENTS

NOTIONAL PERIODS OF FIRE RESISTANCE

modified
½ hour   ½ hour   1 hour

---

n l t 21 mm

not less than
175 x 50 mm

9.5 mm plasterboard

20.7

total deadweight of floor
kg/m²

9.5 mm plasterboard — 19.5

or 12.5 mm gypsum plaster — 31.9

or 12.5 mm vermiculite
gypsum plaster — 29.0

existing

---

n l t 21 mm

n l t
175 x 50 mm

timber laths and plaster
not less than 16 mm thick

16

29.4

existing

---

n l t 21 mm

n l t
175 x 50 mm

12.5 mm fibre insulating board

20.2

12.5 mm gypsum plaster — 31.4

existing

---

n l t 21 mm

n l t
175 x 50 mm

12.5 mm plasterboard

23.4

5 mm gypsum plaster — 28.0

29

Note that 3-storeys is the permitted limit for a building with timber floors which is converted to PG III use.*
Note that 2-storeys is the limit for timber framed external walls within 1 m of the relevant boundary for a PG III building.
Note that 3-storeys is the limit for a timber common stair (new work only).
Any separating wall (in a PG I or PG III) must have not less than 1 hour fire resistance.
It is possible to apply for dispensation or relaxation of these limits.

*(Note that new PG III buildings are permitted up to 4-storeys, with timber floors).

PARTITIONS

It may be necessary in the following cases, to construct fire-resistant internal partitions, in order to separate a stairway from adjacent rooms:
No change of use: stair to new room or rooms in an attic (3-storey) Purpose Group I $\frac{1}{2}$ hour enclosure.
Change of use: a common stair giving access to flats or maisonettes in a house converted to PG III (2- or 3-storeys) 1 hour enclosure.
$\frac{1}{2}$ hour and 1 hour fire resistance can be provided by timber stud-frame partitions clad each side with sheet materials. No wet construction is required.

Schedule 8 Part VII (B) in the Building Regulations lists several constructions. The timber studs should not be less than 50 × 75 mm (2 in × 3 in) at not more than 450 mm centres (18 in). In addition to the constructions listed in Schedule 8, there are several proprietary partition panels which can be used to gain an extra inch or so of room width compared with stud partitions. However, the dimensional variety of old houses is unsuited to the use of factory-made panel components.

Note that wood-based sheet materials can provide fire protection to a stud partition, although of course they add to the total combustibility of a building.
(From 'Fire and timber in modern building design'
by L. A. Ashton. TRADA publication, 1970)

Estimation of contribution of lining materials to fire resisting construction.

3.2 mm	hardboard	5 minutes		
6.4 „	plywood	10 „		
9.5 „	„	15 „	9.5 mm plasterboard 12 minutes	
12.7 „	fibre insulation board	15 „		
12.7 „	medium panelboard	15 „	12.7 „ „ 18 „	
12.7 „	chipboard	20 „		
22.0 „	„	30 „		

However, the use of these materials is limited by Regulation E15 'Surface flamespread' (see p 31). The periods of fire resistance shown are not additive, ie the contribution of two or more materials used together will not usually be the sum of the individual periods because the second layer is subjected to a higher initial temperature than the first.
This is not the case with non-combustible materials such as plasterboard:
2 layers of 9.5 mm plasterboard 28 minutes
2 „ „ 12.7 „ „ 47 „
9.5 + 12.7 mm „ 37 „
These periods can be improved by incorporating wire mesh between the 2 layers to act as stiffening.
Note: Asbestos-cement sheet of the dense type should not be used for fire-resistant partitions because it shatters when heated. Asbestos insulation board (density less than 880 kg/m³ or asbestos wallboard (density 880 to 1440 kg/m³) can be used.
The presence of a mineral-wool quilt (not glass-fibre) in the construction will improve its fire resistance.

DOORS

Any openings in fire-resistant partitions should be protected by self-closing $\frac{1}{2}$ hour fire-check doors:
½ hour fire-check doors can be brought from several manufacturers, made to BS 459 Part 3, 44 mm thick or to other satisfactory tested designs.
The cost varies from £10 to £30 depending on the type of finish and ironmongery. Rising-butt hinges are permitted as the self-closing device required in Regulation E11 (3) (a).

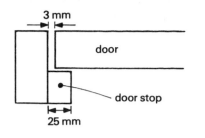

3 mm

door

door stop

25 mm

The clearance between door and frame should be 'as small as is reasonably practicable' (Regulation EII(6)(b)). 3 mm ($\frac{1}{8}$ in) is a reasonable maximum with a 25 mm planted door stop.

Existing panel doors can be improved to $\frac{1}{2}$ hour fire-check standard as follows: infill the panels flush with the framing on each face with 9 or 12 mm thick panelboard securely pinned to the door and screwed through to the opposite panelboard infill. 3.2 mm standard hardboard is then cut and fixed to each side of the door. The finished thickness should be not less than 44 mm and the frame should have 25 mm rebates closely fitting to the door face.
(Ref. Technical Bulletin TB 11/72 'FIDOR' Fibre Building Board Development Organisation).

RESTRICTION OF SURFACE FLAMESPREAD WALLS AND CEILINGS

Regulation E15 applies to new work in improvements ('No change of use') and conversions ('Change of use'). It restricts the use of materials as wall and ceiling linings inside rooms, based on the methods of test in BS 476 Part 7: 1971 'Surface spread of flame tests for materials'. The classification is as follows:

Class 0 — see below
  ,, 1 — surfaces of very low flamespread
  ,, 2 — ,,   ,, low flamespread
  ,, 3 — ,,   ,, medium ,,
  ,, 4 — ,,   ,, rapid   ,,

Class 0, the highest, applies to a material which is either non-combustible throughout (eg brick, concrete, stone, plaster) or has an index of performance I not exceeding 12 and a sub-index i_1 not exceeding 6 when tested in accordance with BS 476 Part 6: 1968, 'Fire propagation test for materials'. Plasterboard achieves Class 0 because the paper facing is bonded throughout to the non-combustible substrate of gypsum plaster, and achieves the required limits of I and i_1. Also, it now must be Class 1 as to surface spread of flame (Building Regulations 1976).

The requirements are shown below. (The material must have a rating not worse than that shown, e.g. Class 1 means that Class 1 or Class 0 material can be used).

	small rooms less than 4 m² floor area	other rooms	circulation spaces
PG I not exceeding 2-storeys	Class 3	wall-Class 1* ceiling-Class 3	wall-Class 1* ceiling-Class 3
PG I exceeding 2-storeys	Class 3	Class 1	Class 0*
PG III any number of storeys	Class 3	Class 1*	Class 0*

*Note: parts of a wall surface can be less than this but not worse than Class 3, provided their total area does not exceed $\frac{1}{2}$ the room's floor area or 20 m², whichever is the lesser. These areas of wall are additional to the areas of doors, windows and their frames.

There is a relaxation for single sheet plastics roof lights in PG III rooms and circulation spaces, and in PG I circulation spaces: if the roof light area does not exceed 2.5 m², and is not less than 3.5 m² from any other roof light, then its flamespread rating can be not lower than Class 3.

MATERIALS

Class 4 — Not to be used on walls and ceilings

— softwood or hardwood less than 400 kg/m³ density (eg western red cedar, balsa).

— fibre insulation board in an untreated state.

Class 3

—softwood or hardwood more than 400 kg/m³ density (ie almost every timber species).

— plywood, chipboard, hardboards and medium boards in an untreated state or decorated with ordinary gloss or emulsion paints.

— acrylic sheet.

— plastics laminates.

(Class 2 not used in buildings)

Class 1

— softwoods or hardwoods (density >400 kg/m³) treated with one of methods A, B, C (see below).

— plywood, chipboard or fibre building boards treated with B or C (some plywoods can be treated with A).

— manufactured 'flame-retardant' grades of plywood, chipboard, strawboard and fibre building boards.

— 'flame-retardant' grade plastics laminate.

— mineral-wool quilt, slab or mat.

— sprayed or brushed plastics finish on non-combustible substrate.

Class 0

— brick, concrete, stone, plaster exposed or decorated with wallpaper or paints.

— plasterboard decorated with wallpaper or paints.

— asbestos-cement sheet.

— metal sheet, aluminium foil.

— **'Kinken' or 'Delignit FRCW' brands of wood-based sheets.**

— plywood, chipboard or hardboard decorated with 'Lurimail CL' and 'Lurifuge' clear varnish or with 'Lurieflame retardant emulsion B12' — **recently introduced by Benbow Fire Protection, Old Woods Trading Estate, Torquay, Devon. (now owned by J. W. Bolton of Beckenham, Kent).**

Note: these products are water-based and therefore should not be used in wet areas.

— **plywood impregnated with 'Retroflame' made by Robinson Carpet Processing Co Ltd, Weston-super-Mare. (now Retroflame Ltd., Oldmixon Crescent, Winterstoke Rd., Weston-super-Mare).**

METHODS OF TREATMENT TO GIVE CLASS 1

A Vacuum/pressure impregnation carried out in special treatment plants. Suitable for softwood, hardwood and some plywoods.

products — 'Celure F'
    — 'Rentokil flameproof'   } Rentokil Laboratories Ltd
    — 'Oxylene'   The Timber Fireproofing Co Ltd
    — 'Pyrolith'   Hicksons Timber Impregnation
    — **Fireprufe**   Co Ltd
    — **Retroflame**

B Clear surface finishes can be applied on site.

— 'Albi clear'   Rentokil Ltd

— 'Pyromors transparent'   Carson-Paripan Ltd **Also, Lurifuge.**

Note that a material treated by method A can be finished with an ordinary non flame retardant clear finish, without losing its Class 1 rating.

C Paints can be applied on site.

— 'Albi-R' and 'Albisaf'   Rentokil Ltd

— Brolac fire retardant emulsion   Berger Paints

— Camrex intumescent matt finish
— Camrex intumescent gloss finish } Camrex Holdings Ltd

— Coatostone liquid stone paint
— C and R fire retardant emulsion } Craig & Rose Ltd

— Cockade flame retardant emulsion
— Cockade flame retardant enamel } Federated Paints Ltd

— Dinaphon V103   Storry Smithson & Co Ltd

— Pyrockeck f r emulsion
— Pyrocheck Snuff } The Beaver Group

— Fireguard flame retardant emulsion   Redaluma Paint Co Ltd

— Granyte flame retardant emulsion   W. W. Hill, Son & Wallace

— Hadrian Retaflam retardant emulsion   Smith & Walton Ltd

— Hydromat flame retardant emulsion   The United Paint Co Ltd

- 'Taf' 'Trerock'   Pearl Paints Ltd
- Mander's f r F P paint   Manders Paints Ltd
- Nulon Firetex K205   W. & J. Leigh & Co
- Oxylene PVA f r emulsion   The Timber Fireproofing Co Ltd
- *Timonox flame retardant emulsion } Associated Lead
- *Timonox satin lustre   Manufacturers Ltd
- Timonox Flocoat f r emulsion
- TKS firecheck   Turner King & Shepherd Ltd

*available retail

Manufacturers' instructions must be carefully followed.

Inclusion of a trade-name in these lists does not denote approval by TRADA, nor does omission of a trade-name imply disapproval.

Ordinary paints and clear finishes:

Most decorative finishes (with the exception of nitro-cellulose lacquers or similar, which should not be used) do not downgrade the flamespread performance of the substrate material. Some of these finishes are misleadingly described as 'flame-retardant'. They should not be confused with genuine flame retardant finishes (tables B and C on previous page) which improve the performance of a material to Class 1 rating.

Expanded polystyrene tiles cannot be tested for surface flamespread due to their low melting point. Although Regulation E15 does not apply to existing wall and ceiling surfaces (even when there is a change of use from PG I to PG III) it is still good sense to remove any expanded polystyrene tiles which are not attached with overall adhesive.

Attic conversion

6

In many old houses the attic space is capable of being converted into 'habitable' rooms (bedroom, living-room, study etc). This is often the easiest and cheapest way of extending the accommodation in a house and has other advantages:

fig. 1

— existing structure and cladding

— no loss of outdoor space

— best sunlight/daylight

— best views

— Town Planning permission not required, except where dormer window(s) or roof extension(s) are proposed.

Building Regulations

*These figures relate to 3-storey private houses. For 4 or more storey houses the loads are 1.5 kN/m² (153 kg/m² – 31.3 lb/ft²).

Building Regulations approval is required: all 'new work' must comply with Parts B to P. The attic floor is considered to be 'new work' since accommodation is being provided where there was none before: therefore, under Part D, it must be capable of carrying an imposed load of 1.44 kN/m² (146 kg/m² — 30 lb/ft²)*, and, under Part E, must have ½ hour fire resistance in a PG I house not exceeding 4-storeys or modified ½ hour in a PG I bungalow. Thermal insulation of the roof is required to comply with Part F — 'U' value not more than 0.60 w/m²/°C (see Building Regulations 1976).

The prime limitation on attic conversion is usually the existing attic size and the house layout below: in other words, is the attic big enough and can a stair be fitted into the rooms below? The stair must comply with Part H (see chapter on Stairs). Note that a 'loft-ladder' and trapdoor is not permitted for attic accommodation — except when it is used for storage purposes only. In situations where Part H would be impractical, application for relaxation of the Regulations should be made.

Procedure

The first item to check is the existing attic headroom; Regulation K8 'Height of habitable rooms' applies where an attic is converted to 'habitable' room(s). 'Habitable' rooms are bedroom, living-room, dining-room or dining-kitchen but not bathroom, wc, boxroom, passageway or non-dining-kitchen.

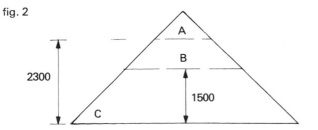

fig. 2

The requirement is that part of the habitable room in a roofspace should be at least 2300 mm (7 ft 6½ in) above the finished floor level (allow for thickness of boarding on top of joists). The area of this part on plan should be at least half the area measured at a height of 1500 mm (4 ft 11½ in).

Area A = not less than $\dfrac{\text{Area B}}{2}$

The length of roof at A is less than that at B in the case of a hipped roof, but the same in the case of a gable roof.

fig. 3

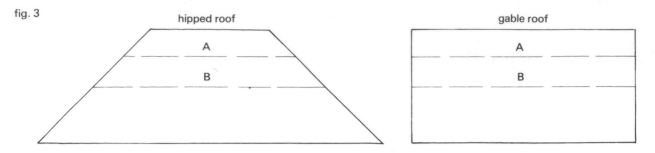

hipped roof

gable roof

A

B

A

B

There is no restriction on the minimum height at C and the floor can touch the sloping roof. However, the floor area determines the window size which must be not less than floor area ÷ 10 in habitable rooms, and the 'ventilator' or opening window size (not less than floor area ÷ 20) in habitable rooms, kitchen, wc or bathroom. It is therefore often advisable to limit the floor width. This will happen anyway where deep purlin/floor beams are used (see p50).

fig. 4

WINDOWS are most easily provided in the gable end wall. This is not possible where the roof is hipped or where the house is in a terrace: In these cases, the choice is between a roof-window or a dormer window.

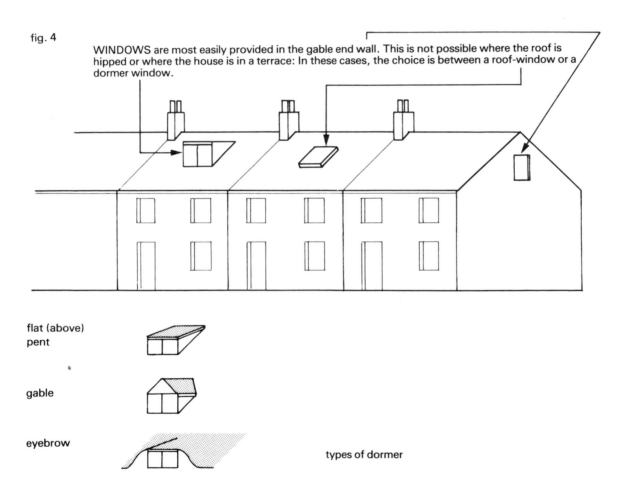

flat (above)
pent

gable

eyebrow

types of dormer

In terms of value-for-money, the roof-window is preferable to the dormer – due to the amount of framing, cladding, insulation and lining involved in the latter, which is usually purpose made by the builder. The addition of a dormer window to an existing roof often produces unsatisfactory junctions of materials, and a reliance on unsightly bituminous felt flashings. By comparison, the roof-window is a sophisticated factory-made unit usually double glazed and with metal flashings supplied cut to shape: the centre-pivot type permits window cleaning from inside. The dormer has the psychological advantage that people like windows to be vertical (for curtain-hanging) and has the physical advantage of increasing the ceiling area at 2300 mm height in order to satisfy

fig. 5

regulation K8. Note that if the window sill is below the 1500 mm level then the increase in A will be partially offset by an increase in B:

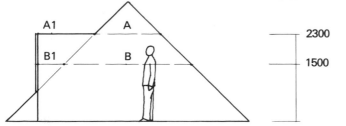

If an increase in A is not required, the ceiling height in the dormer can be less than 2300 mm but not less than 2000 mm (6 ft 7 in). Part of the opening window or vent area must be at least 1750 mm (5 ft 9 in) above the floor.

IS THE ROOFSPACE BIG ENOUGH?

The minimum roofspan required to satisfy Regulation K8 depends on the roofslope: the narrower the span, the steeper the slope must be. This is shown below which assumes that the span and slope do not vary over the proposed area of a habitable room and that the roof is not hipped. The dimensions have been calculated as follows:

fig. 6

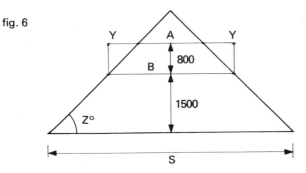

B = not more than 2A (at the limit B = 2A)

$$B = 2Y + A \quad \therefore 2Y + A = 2A \quad \therefore A = 2Y$$

$$Y = \frac{800}{\tan. Z°} \quad \therefore A = \frac{2 \times 800}{\tan. Z°}$$

$$S = A + 2\left(\frac{Y \times 2300}{800}\right) = A + \frac{A \times 23}{8} =$$

3.875A

These are the minimum dimensions required to satisfy K8. If the existing roofspace internal sizes are less than these, then either:

i dormer window(s) will have to be added to increase A

or

ii the room cannot be 'habitable rooms'.

Note:

Internal finished dimensions are required: allowance should be made for the thickness of proposed floorboarding and lining board under the rafters, when measuring the existing structure.

Putting in deeper joists above an existing ceiling will, of course, further reduce the height of roofspace.

fig. 7   Minimum roof dimensions required, for different roof slope angles, to satisfy Regulation K8 'Height of habitable rooms'.

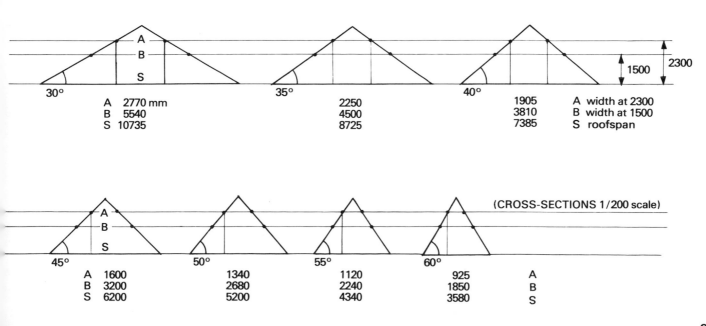

30°		35°	40°	
A	2770 mm	2250	1905	A width at 2300
B	5540	4500	3810	B width at 1500
S	10735	8725	7385	S roofspan

(CROSS-SECTIONS 1/200 scale)

45°		50°	55°	60°	
A	1600	1340	1120	925	A
B	3200	2680	2240	1850	B
S	6200	5200	4340	3580	S

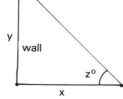

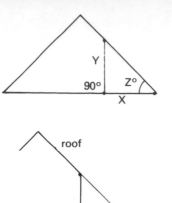

How to find the roofslope angle z°:

a From inside

measure angle using protractor or adjustable set square

or measure lengths x and y then find z° from tangent $z° = y \div x$

x and y can be measured from any convenient point provided that the angle between them is 90°

b From outside

measure angle with a clinometer

or find by eye the point at which the angle of the roofline would meet the ground

measure x and y tangent $z° = y \div x$

tangent 30° = 0.5774

    ,,   35° = 0.7102

    ,,   40° = 0.8391

    ,,   45° = 1.0000

    ,,   50° = 1.1918

    ,,   55° = 1.4281

    ,,   60° = 1.7321   refer to trig tables for other angles

FIRE REGULATIONS AND ATTIC CONVERSION

When there is no 'change of use', the existing building need not be upgraded to comply with the Building Regulations Part E — Structural Fire Precautions, unless any 'new work' adversely affects the existing in relation to Part E. However, this is just what happens with attic conversion which has the effect of adding a storey to a house; reference to table A in Regulation E5 will show that the period of fire resistance required for structural elements increases with the number of storeys. The requirements are summarised as follows:

A Attic conversion of bungalow

fig. 8

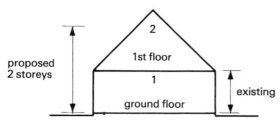

fig. 9

B Attic conversion of 2-storey house to provide two or more rooms

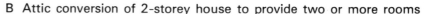

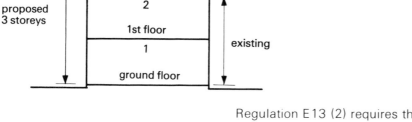

Regulation E13 (2) requires that a PG I house of three (or more) storeys shall have a protected staircase (including any hall or landing associated with the stair and any part of a floor linking stair flights). The requirements for the structure, which separates the stair from all other parts of the building, are:

a Period of fire resistance as stated in Regulation E5 ie $\frac{1}{2}$ hour for a 3-storey house

b Any opening in the structure which gives access to a habitable room or kitchen shall be fitted with a $\frac{1}{2}$ hour fire door complying with Regulation E11:

Regulation E11 (5)

a Single leaf door, single swing only

or

Double leaf door, each leaf of which swings in the opposite direction to the other

b Freedom from collapse for not less than 30 minutes and resistance to passage of flame for not less than 20 minutes, but no minimum period of insulation. A $\frac{1}{2}$ hour 'fire-check' door.

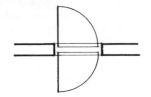

(5) Any door shall be fitted with an automatic self-closing device: rising butt hinges are permitted in this case.

(6) No part of the hinge shall be of combustible material or non-combustible material with a melting-point less than 800°C (this rules out nylon or aluminium).

(7) If two separate doors are installed the required fire resistance can be achieved by both together or by either of them separately.

Note:
THESE REQUIREMENTS APPLY TO ALL DOORS TO HABITABLE ROOMS AND KITCHEN FROM THE STAIRWAY IN EACH STOREY OF THE HOUSE.

Refer to the chapter 'Fire precautions' for typical constructions of doors and stud partitions. Existing walls of 100 mm (4 in) thickness brickwork provide up to two hours fire-resistance, plastered or unplastered, loadbearing or non-loadbearing.

Where an existing stair rises directly from a habitable room (eg a sitting-room), it is not necessary to build a ½ hour separating partition around the stair, provided there is a ½ hour wall between that room and any other habitable room or kitchen and that any doors in that wall are ½ hour, fire-check self-closing. The first floor over this room should be upgraded to provide ½ hour fire resistance.

The new second floor must be ½ hour fire resistant for its whole area. (see chapter 'Fire precautions').

These requirements apply where there are two or more rooms in the third storey.

Where there is only one room proposed, these requirements can be partially relaxed (as stated in DoE circular 67/71 p 8) as follows:

C Attic conversion of 2-storey house to provide one room

a The floor of the new second storey must have full ½ hour fire resistance.

All existing doors in the ground and first storeys to habitable rooms and kitchen from hall and stairwell are to be fitted with self-closing devices (rising butts permitted) and any glazing in the doors to be wired glass.

b In all cases there should be a window in the new room capable of being opened sufficiently to provide an emergency escape.

c Where the new stair from the first storey rises over the existing stair and is within the same enclosure — the new room must be fitted with a ½ hour fire resisting self-closing door set in an enclosure with ½ hour fire resistance.

d Where the new stair rises from the existing stairway through an existing bedroom, it must be separated from that room and the rest of the house by a ½ hour fire resistance enclosure, with a ½ hour fire resistant self-closing door at either top or bottom.

e Where the new stair rises from an existing bedroom the walls and floor of that bedroom must have full ½ hour fire resistance, with a ½ hour fire resistant self-closing door in a ½ hour fire resistant enclosure at the top of the new stair.

f Where access is by a loft-ladder (ie where the new room is not a habitable room) the hatch must be ½ hour fire resistant self-closing or there must be ½ hour fire resistant self-closing door and ½ hour fire resistant enclosure at the top.

g Subject to d and e, the existing first floor must have at least modified ½ hour fire resistance.

STRENGTH OF EXISTING TIMBERS

Old timbers have the same structural capacity as new timbers of the same size and species, unless they have been attacked by fungus or insect in which case replacement may be necessary. Old ceiling joists tend to be square in section and thus have greater strength than the equivalent modern joist of the same depth. Example: 100 x 100 mm joists at 600 mm centres (4 in x 4 in at 24 in) have the same loadbearing capacity as 50 x 100 mm joists at 300 mm centres (2 in x 4 in at 12 in centres).

Existing ceiling joists are almost certainly incapable of supporting a superimposed floor loading of 1.44 kN/m² (146 kg/m²—30 lb/ft²)* Refer to Schedule 6 Table 1, the Building Regulations for floor joist span-charts. The joists also have to carry an increased dead load (ie floorboards). The total dead load of a floor with one hour fire resistance is approximately 31 kg/m².

The total dead load of a floor with ½ hour fire resistance is approximately 27 kg/m².

*These figures relate to 3-storey private houses. For 4 or more storey houses the loads are 1.5 kN/m² (153 kg/m² — 31.3 lb/ft²).

The total dead load of a floor with modified $\frac{1}{2}$ hour fire resistance is approximately 24 kg/m² (See constructions in the chapter 'Fire precautions').

A Doubling of existing joists
Where the span is short and the ceiling joists relatively deep, it may be possible to add joists of the same depth thus sharing the increased load.

fig. 10

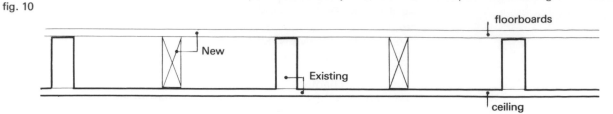

floorboards
New
Existing
ceiling

Note. The example given is a typical one. The maximum spans in Schedule 6 have been changed in the Building Regulations 1976 but this does not affect the method explained. The total load on the floor is the sum of the dead and live loads.

Example: existing joists 150 mm deep at 600 mm centres (6 in at 24 in). Add 50 x 150 mm joists. The floorboards are thus supported at 300 mm centres. $\frac{1}{2}$ hour construction (dead load 27 kg/m²) from Schedule 6 Table 1; 50 x 150 mm floor joists at 400 mm centres will span 3.23 m. Floor joists at 300 mm centres therefore have a loading safety-margin of 400 ÷ 300 = 1.33 and so could carry loads up to 170 x 1.33 = 226 kg/m² over this span. Note that this increase cannot be applied to the span (ie 50 x 150 mm joists at 300 mm centres cannot safely support 170 kg/m² over a span of 3.23 x 4/3), without exceeding the maximum permitted deflection (0.003 x span).

The joist depths and spans shown in Schedule 6 Table 1 are within this limit. The calculation is as follows:

$$\text{Maximum deflection} = \frac{5}{384} \times \frac{WL^3}{EI} = 0.003L$$

$$\therefore L^2 = \frac{0.003 \times 384 \times EI}{5W}$$

W = Total load on beam (kg) = load per cm run x L
L = Span in cm
E (mean value) = 84,600 kg/cm² (S2 group softwood)

$$I = \frac{bd^3}{12} \quad b = \text{breadth of joist (cm)} \quad d = \text{depth of joist (cm)}$$

Example: 5 cm x 15 cm joists at 30 cm centres

$$I = \frac{5 \times 15^3}{12}, \text{ Total floor loading } 170 \text{ kg/m}^2 = \frac{170}{10,000} \text{kg/cm}^2$$

$$\therefore \text{ load per cm run of beam is } \frac{170}{10,000} \times 30 = \frac{51}{100} = 0.51 \text{ kg}$$

$$\therefore L^2 = \frac{0.003 \times 384 \times 84,600 \times 5 \times 15^3}{5 \times 0.51 \times L \times 12}$$

$$\therefore L^3 = \frac{0.003 \times 32 \times 84,600 \times 3375}{0.51} = \frac{96 \times 84.6 \times 3375}{0.51}$$

L = 377.3 cm = 3.773 m

In this particular example the increased span ratio made possible, as a result of having joists at 300 mm centres instead of 400 mm is 3.773 ÷ 3.12 = 1.2 (compare with 1.33 increased load permitted). The smaller the joist depth, then the more critical is deflection in limiting the span.

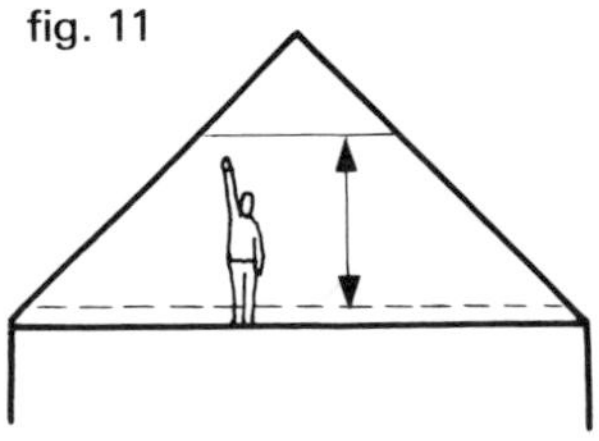

Where the existing joists are not strong enough to carry the increased loading, consider the alternatives:

B Where headroom is not critical, floor joists of the required depth can be put in between the existing joists without disturbing the ceiling below. It is essential to leave a gap of at least 6 mm ($\frac{1}{4}$ in) to prevent any load being put on the existing ceiling:

fig. 11

fig. 12

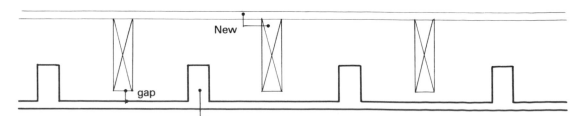

New
gap
Existing

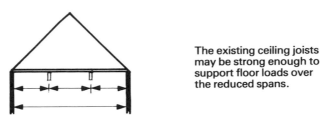

Floor joist sizes can be read directly from Schedule 6 Table 1, Building Regulations. The dead load is less than 25 kg/m² as there is no ceiling load on the new joists.

C Where attic headroom is critical, or where it is not possible to fit new floor joists onto the existing wallplate, more radical methods are required, as below:

Reduce the joist span by putting in a beam (or beams) below the existing ceiling.

fig. 13

— joist

— wallplate

fig. 14

Beam

New span   New span

Existing span

The existing ceiling joists may be strong enough to support floor loads over the reduced spans.

This method is suitable for terrace houses with loadbearing separating walls. The provision of a new staircase into the attic will affect the position of the new beam(s) (see chapter 'Stairs'). The beam can be of steel, reinforced concrete or timber. Timber beams offer certain advantages in improvement work:

1 Lighter in weight than steel or reinforced concrete of the same length and load, therefore easier to manoeuvre through doors or windows etc, and to put into position.

2 Workability — easy to cut to size and to fix.

3 Choice of sizes (different species have different strengths).

The rest of this leaflet deals with timber beams.

Regulation K8 requires 2 m (6 ft 7 in) headroom below a beam in a habitable room.

fig. 15

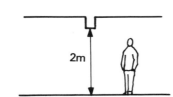

2m

FIRE RESISTANCE

A timber beam will burn on the surface, but the core retains its structural strength, unlike steel which twists and collapses. The 'charring rate' for any structural timber is approximately 0.64 mm per minute (approximately 1″ in 40 minutes) off each exposed surface.

TABLE 1 NOTIONAL RATE OF CHARRING FOR THE CALCULATION OF RESIDUAL SECTION

Species	Charring in 30 min	Charring in 1 hour
	mm	mm
1 Species having densities* less than 420 kg/m³	25	50
2 Species having densities of 420 kg/m³ or more (except where noted)	20	40
3 Oak, utile, keruing (gurjun), teak, greenheart, jarrah	15	30

*Density at 18 per cent moisture content
Note: Linear interpolation is permissible between the values given.

Example: 50 x 150 mm beam supporting floor.
After ½ hour's burning, the effective structural depth will be 150 — approximately (0.64 x 30) = 131 mm and breadth will be 75 — approximately (0.64 x 30) x 2 = 37 mm.

fig. 16

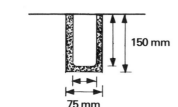

150 mm

75 mm

It is therefore possible to 'oversize' the timber beam to allow a 'sacrificial' margin, the thickness of which depends on the required period of fire resistance. This will permit the beam to be exposed under a

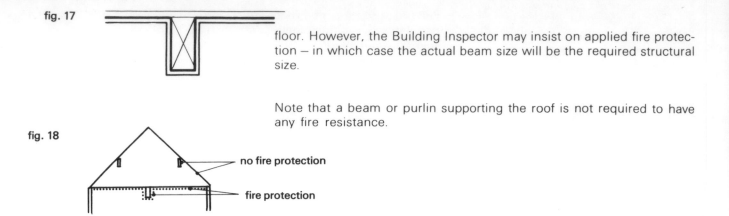

fig. 17

floor. However, the Building Inspector may insist on applied fire protection — in which case the actual beam size will be the required structural size.

Note that a beam or purlin supporting the roof is not required to have any fire resistance.

fig. 18

no fire protection

fire protection

TIMBER BEAM DESIGN

There are so many variable factors that it is difficult to give actual beam sizes here. The suggested procedure is:

1 Determine the maximum safe span of the existing joists to carry the proposed floor loading. This will decide the number of beams required.

2 Determine the load on each beam: (floor area supported by beam x total floor load) + any partition loads (see p 61).

fig. 19

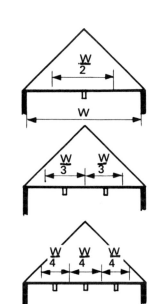

1 beam

a central beam supports $\frac{W}{2}$ **x the beam length**

2 beams

Each beam supports $\frac{W}{3}$ **x the beam length**

3 beams

Each beam supports $\frac{W}{4}$ **x the beam length**

fig. 20

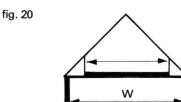

Note that the actual floor width is less than W if side partitions are put in:

3 Divide the load carried by the beam-span to find the load/metre run of beam.

4 Assume a beam-width (eg 50, 75 or 100 mm). Divide the load/metre run by the beam-width in centimetres (10 millimetres) to find the 'unit distributed load'/m run/cm width.

5 This value (kg/m/cm) can be used directly on the TRADA 'span-charts for solid timber beams' (published October, 1968), for whichever timber species is selected. In view of the probable spans and loads involved, and the limitations on beam depth due to headroom, the likeliest timbers are tropical hardwoods. Keruing is one of the most readily available hardwoods in structural sizes, although stronger hardwoods are available (eg greenheart, karri, opepe, ekki).

It is assumed that there is no load sharing between beams (therefore the minimum value for 'E' is taken) and that the floor load is long-term loading.

The span-chart on p43 relates to keruing 65 grade, air dry.

SPAN CHART FOR BEAM KERUING 65 GRADE, AIR DRY
FLOOR LOADING 175 kg/m². (145 LIVE + 30 DEAD)

Keruing 65 grade, air dry: $E \div 10^6 = 0.931$ N/cm² (minimum value, no load-sharing). Bending stress = 1241 N/cm² (long term load, no load-sharing). Shear stress = 165.5 N/cm² (no load-sharing).

		WIDTH OF FLOOR SUPPORTED				
*floor width × 175 kg/m² ÷ 5 =		1m (35.0)	1.5 (52.5)	2.0 (70.0)	2.5 (87.5)	3.0 (105.0)
	50 mm × 150	2.6	2.25	2.05	1.90	1.80
	× 175	3.0	2.65	2.40	2.25	2.10
	× 200	3.4	3.00	2.75	2.50	2.40
beam size	× 225	3.8	3.40	3.10	2.85	2.70
width × depth	× 250	4.3	3.75	3.40	3.15	3.00
	× 275	4.7	4.15	3.80	3.50	3.30
	× 300	5.2	4.50	4.10	3.80	3.60
*floor width × 175 kg/m² ÷ 7.5 =		(23.33)	(35.0)	(46.6)	(58.3)	(70.0)
	75 mm × 150	2.95	2.60	2.35	2.20	2.05
or 2 × 38 mm	× 175	3.40	3.00	2.70	2.50	2.40
bolted together	× 200	3.90	3.40	3.10	2.90	2.75
bolts at 600 mm	× 225	4.40	3.80	3.50	3.25	3.10
centres	× 250	5.00	4.30	3.90	3.60	3.40
	× 275	5.50	4.70	4.35	4.00	3.80
	× 300	6.00	5.20	4.70	4.35	4.10
*floor width × 175 kg/m² ÷ 10 =		(17.5)	(26.25)	(35.0)	(43.75)	(52.5)
	100 mm × 150	3.25	2.80	2.60	2.40	2.25
or 2 × 50 mm	× 175	3.80	3.30	3.00	2.80	2.65
bolted together	× 200	4.30	3.80	3.40	3.20	3.00
bolts at 600 mm	× 225	4.85	4.20	3.80	3.60	3.40
centres	× 250	5.40	4.70	4.30	4.00	3.75
	× 275	6.00	5.20	4.70	4.40	4.15
	× 300	6.60	5.70	5.20	4.80	4.50

*The values in brackets are the 'unit distributed loads' on 1 m length and 1 cm width of each beam. This value is used on the 'TRADA span-charts for solid timber beams', for whichever timber is selected.

Example:

fig. 21

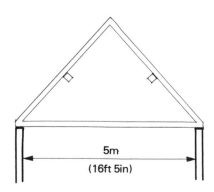

5m
(16ft 5in)

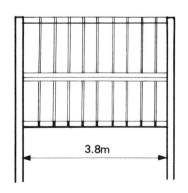

3.8m

Existing ceiling — joists 50 × 125 × 400 mm centres from Table 1 in Schedule 6 of the Building Regulations, the maximum span for these with 175 kg/m² total floor loading = 2.61 m.
Putting in a beam at centre span will reduce the joist span to 2.5 m, thus permitting the existing ceiling joists to be used as floor joists.

fig. 22

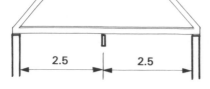

Required beam span, for example, 3.8 m (12 ft 6 in). Look under 2.5 m column heading in span-chart on p43.

a 50 x 300 mm beam in keruing 65 grade, air dry

or b 75 mm x 275 mm (or 2 x 38 mm x 275 mm bolted together)

or c 100 mm x 250 mm (or 2 x 50 mm x 250 mm bolted together)

The choice of size depends on:

1 Available headroom under beam (not less than 2 m permitted)

2 Availability of timber sizes

3 Economy: cost is related to the cross-sectional area of timber

a 50 x 300 = 0.015 m²

b 75 x 275 = 0.0206 m²

c 100 x 250 = 0.025 m²

a is cheaper than b or c

4 Deadweight of timber to be lifted by hand; density of keruing is 720 kg/m³.

a volume 0.05 x 0.3 x 3.8 = 0.057 m³ x 720 = 41 kg (90 lb)

b volume 0.075 x 0.275 x 3.8 = 0.078 x 720 = 56 kg (123 lb)

c volume 0.10 x 0.25 x 3.8 = 0.095 x 720 = 68 kg (150 lb)

Two men can safely carry and lift approximately 70 kg (155 lb) b and c can be divided into weights of 2 x 28 kg and 2 x 34 kg.

Note in the case of double beams it is not advisable to separate these into two beams as they would have to carry a heavier total load.

fig. 23

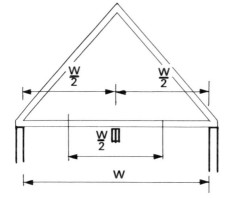
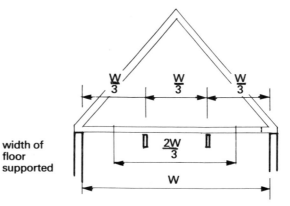

width of floor supported

FLOORBOARDS

The span-chart on p 45 compares the thicknesses of softwood boards, chipboard and plywood. Note that as the board span increases so the load on each joist increases.

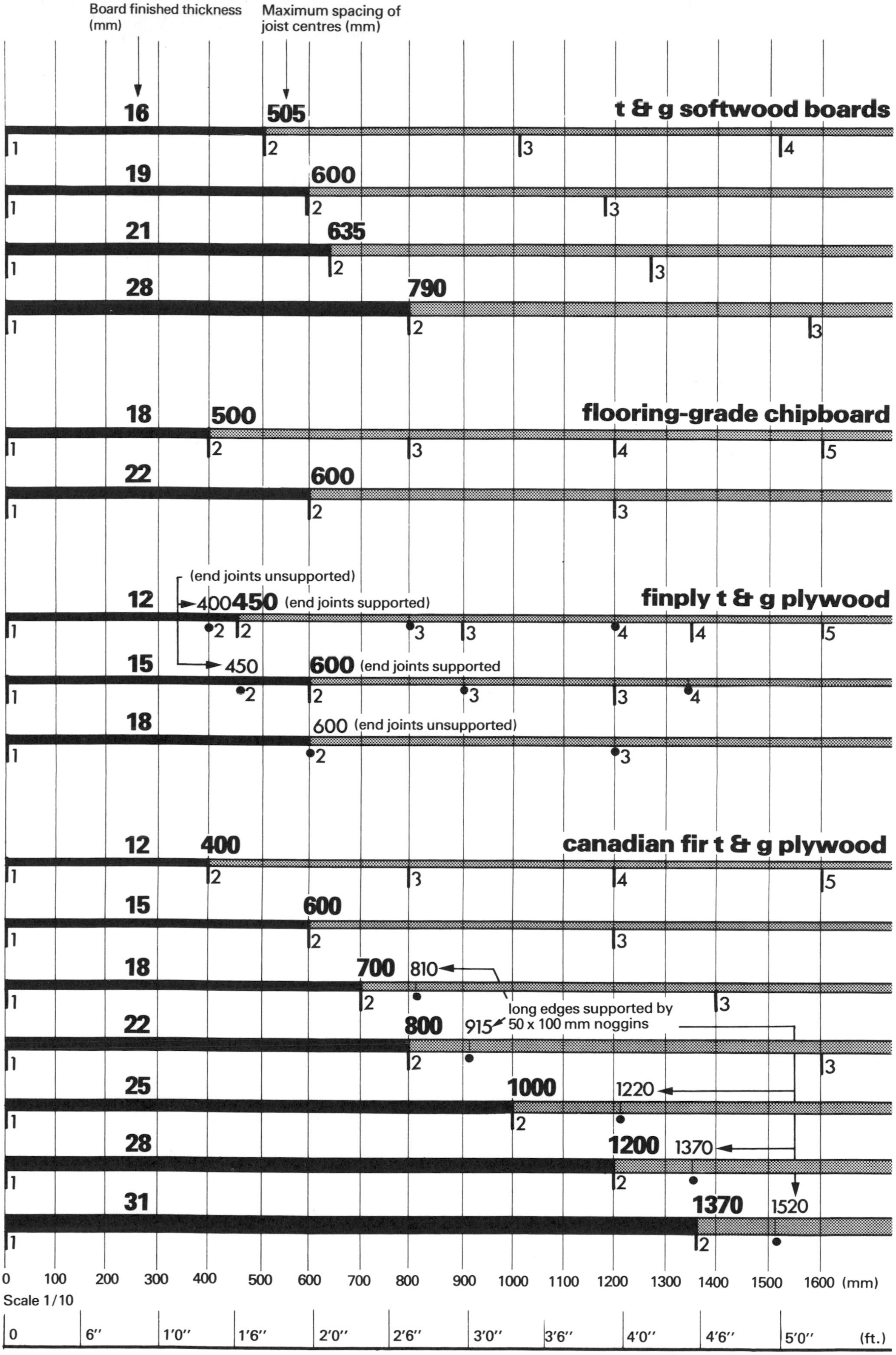

Board finished thickness (mm)

Maximum spacing of joist centres (mm)

t & g softwood boards

16	505
1 · 2 · 3 · 4

| 19 | 600 |
1 · 2 · 3

| 21 | 635 |
1 · 2 · 3

| 28 | 790 |
1 · 2 · 3

flooring-grade chipboard

| 18 | 500 |
1 · 2 · 3 · 4 · 5

| 22 | 600 |
1 · 2 · 3

finply t & g plywood

(end joints unsupported)

| 12 | 400 450 | (end joints supported) |
1 · •2 · 2 · •3 · 3 · •4 · 4 · 5

| 15 | → 450 | 600 (end joints supported |
1 · •2 · 2 · •3 · 3 · •4

| 18 | 600 (end joints unsupported) |
1 · •2 · •3

canadian fir t & g plywood

| 12 | 400 |
1 · 2 · 3 · 4 · 5

| 15 | 600 |
1 · 2 · 3

| 18 | 700 | 810 ← |
1 · 2 · • · 3

long edges supported by 50 x 100 mm noggins

| 22 | 800 | 915 |
1 · 2 · • · 3

| 25 | 1000 | 1220 ← |
1 · 2 · •

| 28 | 1200 | 1370 ← |
1 · 2 · •

| 31 | 1370 | 1520 |
1 · 2 · •

| 0 | 100 | 200 | 300 | 400 | 500 | 600 | 700 | 800 | 900 | 1000 | 1100 | 1200 | 1300 | 1400 | 1500 | 1600 | (mm) |

Scale 1/10

| 0 | 6'' | 1'0'' | 1'6'' | 2'0'' | 2'6'' | 3'0'' | 3'6'' | 4'0'' | 4'6'' | 5'0'' | (ft.) |

Long span softwood decking

This is a type of flooring used in North America (and in Britain in the Middle Ages — although oak and elm were used then). It reduces the overall floor structure thickness by several inches, compared with the usual joist-and-board floor, and so it can be very useful in attic situations where headroom is critical. The following table shows in column e the reduction in depth:

*It is likely that stress graded timber (to BS 4978) will be more readily available and therefore this should be borne in mind when considering such long span softwood decking.

t & g boards in redwood/whitewood 50 grade single span *		16 mm t & g boards on joists at 400 mm centres		
a	b	c	d	e
Board thickness (mm)	Limit of span (m) (deflection not more than 0.003 × span)	Joist size for span b (mm)	Total depth board & joist (mm)	d − a (mm)
38	1.39	38 x 100	116	78 (3″)
50	1.93	38 x 125	141	91 (3½″)
63	2.52	38 x 150	166	103 (4″)
75	3.05	38 x 175	191	116 (4½″)

The permitted spans shown in column b can be increased, if the boards are continuous over two or more spans:

Continuous span

Board thickness	Limit of span
38	1.87
50	2.60
63	3.38
75	4.10

There should be no end joints between boards in the two span condition. However, in a three span condition it is possible to have end joints, provided these occur over supports and are staggered:

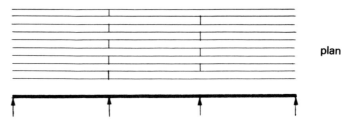

plan

The required fire protection for the floor can be easily provided by fixing sheet materials to the underside of the boards:

fig. 24

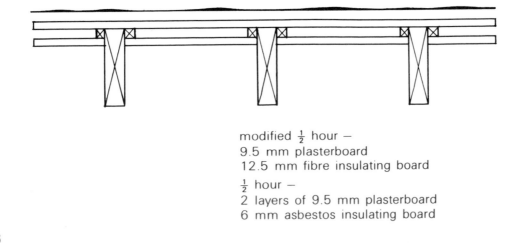

modified ½ hour —
9.5 mm plasterboard
12.5 mm fibre insulating board

½ hour —
2 layers of 9.5 mm plasterboard
6 mm asbestos insulating board

12.5 mm fibre insulating board + 12.5 mm gypsum plaster
12.5 mm plasterboard + 5 mm gypsum plaster
9.5 mm plasterboard + 12.5 mm gypsum plaster

1 hour —
9.5 mm plasterboard + 12.5 mm vermiculite gypsum plaster

The same protection must be given to any supporting beams. Refer to spanchart on p43 for hardwood beam sizes.

INSTALLATION OF TIMBER BEAMS IN EXISTING BUILDING

The main problem is dimensional: is there enough room to get the beam into its required position? The traditional method of building beam-ends into the support walls is not recommended, for several reasons:

1 The beam has to be 150 to 200 mm longer than the room-size in order to give a reasonable bearing surface at each end.
This extra length makes it almost impossible to get the beam in.

fig. 25

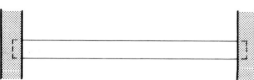

This extra length makes it almost impossible to get the beam in.

2 There may be dampness in the existing wall, thus putting the timber beam at risk.
3 If the beam is housed into a 'separating wall', the fire resistance and the sound insulation will be reduced.

fig. 26

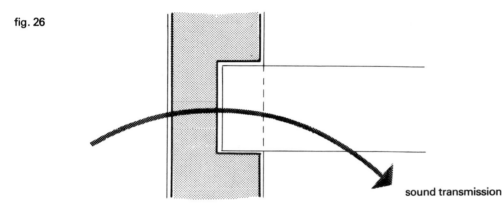

sound transmission

The preferred method is to use metal joist hangers, such as 'Bat SPW welded hanger type S', 2.7 mm galvanised mild steel; bearing surface 89 mm ($3\frac{1}{2}$ in); available in widths of 38, 50, 75, 125, 150 mm and depths of 125, 150, 175, 200, 225 and 250 mm. (Automatic Pressings Ltd).
The 'MAFCO' type W welded steel hanger 10 gauge is available in standard timber sizes (MacAndrews & Forbes).

fig. 27

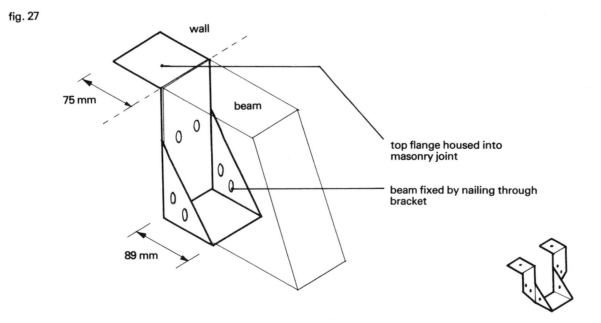

wall

75 mm

beam

top flange housed into masonry joint

beam fixed by nailing through bracket

89 mm

The 'Avon' type 7700 10 gauge joist hanger has two top flanges, thus halving the bearing pressure (see below). (Avon Manufacturing (Warwick) Ltd).

Compared with the traditional method, joist hangers have the following advantages when a beam is put into an existing building:

1 Beam size is actually less than the room size (allowing approximately 6 mm tolerance at each end), thus reducing the cost of material and facilitating installation

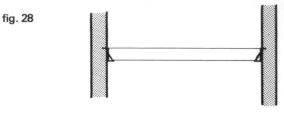

fig. 28

2 Less builders work involved

3 Risk of decay eliminated

4 No reduction in fire resistance or sound insulation of wall.

There is a dimensional problem with joist hangers — the required level of the beam might not coincide with an existing masonry joint.

fig. 29

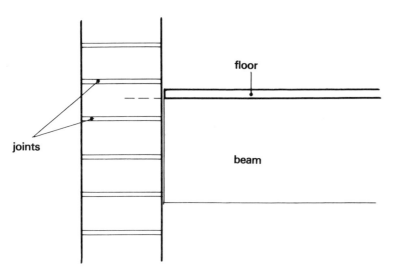

floor

joints

beam

It is permissible to use a hanger with depth slightly less than the beam depth, or to notch the beam:

fig. 30

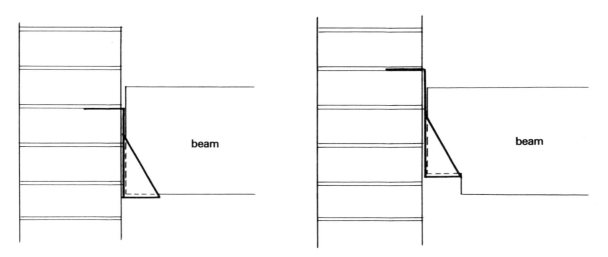

beam

beam

LOAD BEARING: BEAM ON HANGER

Each of the 'SPW' type hangers can support up to 3000 kg (3 tons) if securely clamped in the wall, and with no gap between hanger and wall. The heaviest load in the table on p 50 is 1180 kg (from a 2 No 50 x 300 beam spanning 4.5 m supporting 6.75 m² x 175 kg/m² floor load).

Heavier gauge hangers are available for loads up to 5000 kg. These might be required for the combined roof purlin/floor beam described later.

LOAD BEARING: HANGER ON WALL

The strength of an existing wall is an unknown quantity. Check first that there are no visible defects (cracks, crumbling surface, open joints, dampness etc). Defects must be repaired.

The bearing strength of brickwork or stonework is entirely determined by the mortar joints: hydraulic lime was used as the binding agent for mortar until the late 19th Century, when Portland cement came into common use. Improved types of hydraulic lime were used to some extent from the early 19th Century under names such as Parkers 'Roman cement' (1796), Frost's 'British cement' (1822) and Aspdin's 'Portland cement' (1824), but the factory manufacture of 'modern' Portland cement did not develop until the 1880's. Lime mortar is relatively soft and absorbent and can easily be chipped away from the brick. Cement mortar is hard and impervious, and cannot easily be chipped away.

The basic compressive stress of each brick or stone (when tested separately) is approximately 10 to 15 times as much as the working compressive stress when the units are bonded with cement mortar, or approximately 15 to 40 times as much when cement/lime mortar is used.

The following table shows typical values for modern brickwork (the lowest value for each brick type is shown; values for cement-less mortar are not available; note that the ultimate crushing-strength is far in excess of these values).

Brick	Basic compressive stress. N/mm² set in mortar (mix by volume)		
	1 cement/ 3 sand	1 cement/ 2 lime/ 9 sand	1 cement/ 3 lime/ 12 sand
Engineering class 'A' 70	4.55	2.50	2.05
Engineering class 'B' 49	3.50	2.05	1.70
Fletton 14	1.35	1.00	0.82
London stock 3.5	0.35	0.35	0.25
Handmade facings 7	0.70	0.55	0.49

example:
1180 kg bearing on 75 x 100 mm (flange size of joist hanger)

$$\therefore \text{ Bearing pressure} = \frac{1180}{7500} = 0.158 \text{ kg/mm}^2 = 1.54 \text{ N/mm}^2$$

From the table it can be seen that the flange of the joist hanger should bear onto a brick not worse than Engineering class 'B' in 1:3:12 mortar (or possibly a fletton brick, stronger than the lowest value shown, set in cement mortar). The load can be assumed to spread out below the bearing at an angle of 45°, thus reducing the stress below. The hanger-flange must seat directly onto the brick.

fig. 31

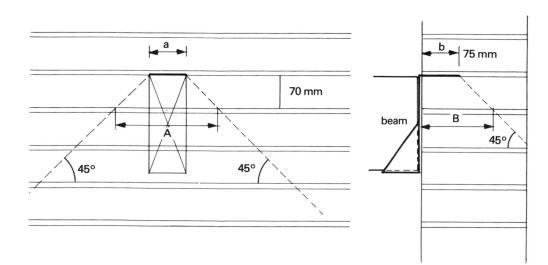

Assume brick thickness to be 70 mm ($2\frac{3}{4}$ in), then $A = a + 140$ mm
$B = b + 70 = 145$ mm
Joist hangers available in 38, 50, 75, 100, 125 and 150 mm widths.

	38	50	75	100	125	150
a	38	50	75	100	125	150
b	75	75	75	75	75	75
(a x b) mm²	2,850	3,750	5,650 (1 brick)	7,500	9,400	11,250
A	178	190	215	240	265	290
B	145	145	145	145	145	145
(A x B) mm²	25,810	27,550	31,175	34,800	38,425	42,050
$\dfrac{A \times B}{a \times b} =$	9.056	7.346	5.517	4.64	4.08	3.73

The final figure shows the factor by which the bearing pressure is reduced through a height of 70 mm. This reduction will continue until the point is reached at which B equals the wall thickness.

In most cases it will be sufficient to insert one engineering brick into the wall to carry the joist hanger, in which case A x B = approx $220 \times 105 = 23000$ mm² (34 in²).

Where the existing wall is of soft brick, soft stone or clay lump, it is advisable to put in at least three courses of engineering brick. Note that the mortar used should approximate to that of the existing wall, otherwise a permanent bond may not be achieved with the surrounding wall.

BEAMS IN THE ROOF SPACE

If headroom below makes it impossible to fit in beams, then they could be fixed above the joists in the attic.

The joists are suspended from the beams by metal framing anchors (eg 'BAT' multi-grip 18 gauge type A or 'MAFCO' Trip-L-Grip type B).

fig. 32

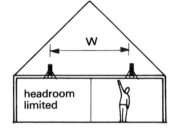

headroom limited

This solution is more limiting since the spacing of the beams is determined by the attic floor width and vice versa. There is also the problem of getting large beams into a roof space, but this can be overcome by using trussed beams or plybox beams made from small timber members which can be assembled in the roof space. Such beams are deeper than solid beams of equivalent load and span, and so the available headroom may be critical, and it may affect the floor width.

The diagram shows that a deep beam spanning between gable walls could support the floor joists and act as a purlin supporting the rafters and form a side wall to the attic room. This depends on the roof geometry (eg a purlin is best placed at rafter mid-span) and particularly on the existing roof structure:

fig. 33

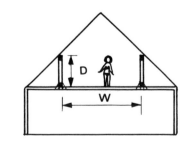

EXISTING ROOF STRUCTURE

A Purlin and rafters

Common in terrace houses with load-bearing separating walls. Where the roof span is more than approximately 4.5 m, it was usual to support the ceiling joists by means of hangers from the purlins, with runners across the joist tops.

Attic conversion may require removing one or both purlins to enable a window or roof light to be put in, or to improve headroom.

fig. 34

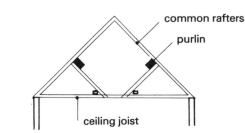

common rafters

purlin

ceiling joist

The function of the purlin varies from roof to roof:

1   fig. 35

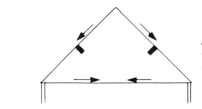

An angled purlin acts solely as a support for the rafters and possibly also for the ceiling joists. Resistance to outward-thrust is provided entirely by the ceiling ties.

2   fig. 36

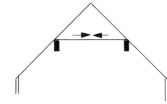

An upright purlin supports the rafters (and possibly the ceiling joists), and can partly resist outward thrust—provided the rafters are notched over the purlin or connected with metal brackets.

3   fig. 37

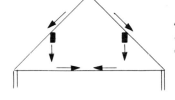

A variation of 2. The tie-members are above the purlin. As with 2, horizontal forces are resolved vertically downwards. It is not necessary to notch the rafters, or to use metal brackets, provided the tie members are securely fixed to the rafters.

4   fig. 38

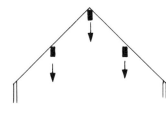

Adding a ridge-purlin eliminates outward thrust, provided the rafters are notched or metal-bracketed to the purlins. No tie members are needed. The simplest way of installing a ridge-purlin into an existing roof is to connect each pair of rafters with a batten (the same section as the rafter) seated onto the purlin (as shown below). Inserting a ridge-purlin should be considered when it is necessary to remove tie members (eg ceiling joists).

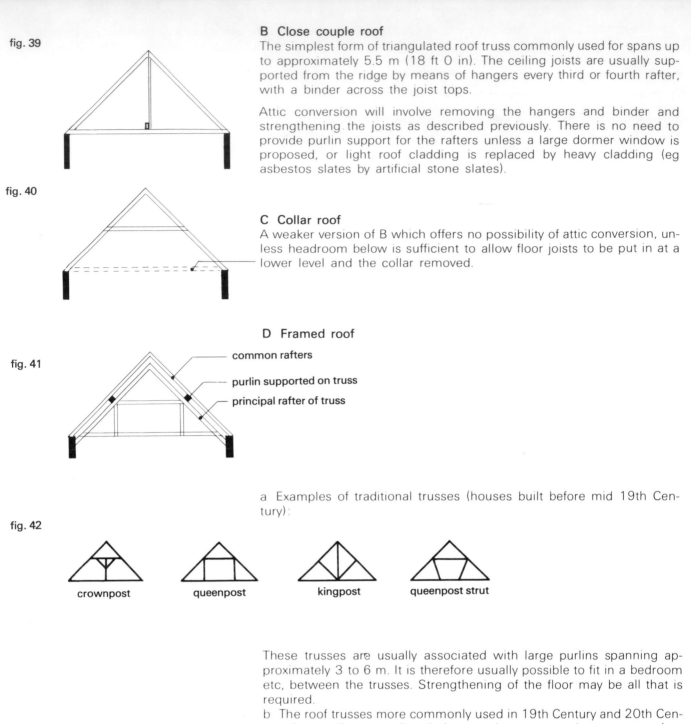

fig. 39

B Close couple roof

The simplest form of triangulated roof truss commonly used for spans up to approximately 5.5 m (18 ft 0 in). The ceiling joists are usually supported from the ridge by means of hangers every third or fourth rafter, with a binder across the joist tops.

Attic conversion will involve removing the hangers and binder and strengthening the joists as described previously. There is no need to provide purlin support for the rafters unless a large dormer window is proposed, or light roof cladding is replaced by heavy cladding (eg asbestos slates by artificial stone slates).

fig. 40

C Collar roof

A weaker version of B which offers no possibility of attic conversion, unless headroom below is sufficient to allow floor joists to be put in at a lower level and the collar removed.

D Framed roof

fig. 41

common rafters

purlin supported on truss

principal rafter of truss

a Examples of traditional trusses (houses built before mid 19th Century):

fig. 42

crownpost   queenpost   kingpost   queenpost strut

These trusses are usually associated with large purlins spanning approximately 3 to 6 m. It is therefore usually possible to fit in a bedroom etc, between the trusses. Strengthening of the floor may be all that is required.

b The roof trusses more commonly used in 19th Century and 20th Century houses have smaller timbers and so are at closer centres (approximately 1 to 3 m). Attic conversion will almost certainly require these trusses to be taken out and deeper purlins put in. A combined purlin/floor beam is ideal, but it must be capable of being fixed before the trusses are taken out (unless temporary support to the rafters can be provided).

c Nearly all house roofs built recently have trussed rafters at 450 mm to 600 mm centres with very small timbers and metal plate connectors. Attic conversion is totally out of the question, as modern roofs are usually low-pitched.

Recommendations: The most suitable method of providing a clear, habitable space in a roof is to change its direction of span from transverse to longitudinal (see p 50).

fig. 43

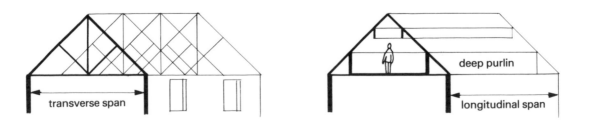

transverse span

deep purlin

longitudinal span

Hipped roof

The deep purlin/floor beam is suitable for roofs with loadbearing cross-walls or gable walls. It is unsuitable for hipped roofs without loadbearing cross-walls, unless a dormer is built out at each end or the roof is converted to a gable-end type. The lack of cross-walls also prevents floor beams being put in to support the floor joists (as suggested on p41).

fig. 44

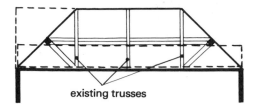

existing trusses

A possible solution for attic conversion of a hipped roof is as follows:
1 Put in transverse beams spanning between loadbearing side walls using metal joist hangers (see p 47).

fig. 45

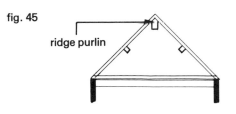

ridge purlin

fig. 46

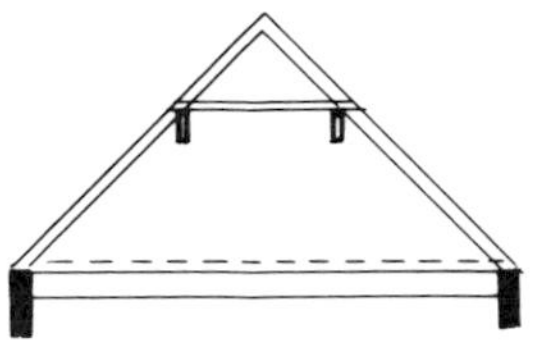

For method of supporting the new purlins see example on p 54
2 Remove existing ceiling joists after ensuring that all horizontal forces from roof are resolved (see p 51 item 3 or item 4)

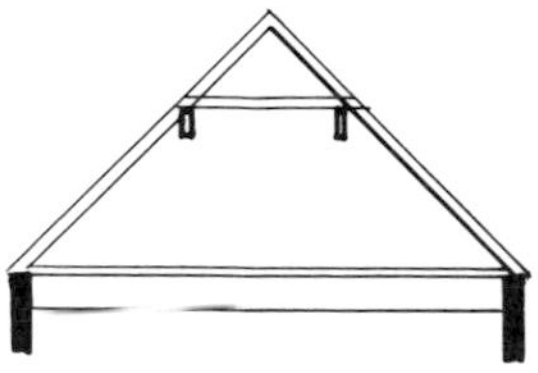

3 Put in long-span timber decking running longitudinally spanning between new transverse beams.

fig. 47

This method offers the following benefits:
a No increased loading is put on the existing roof structure, as the new floor has its own supporting beams.
b There is a gain in attic headroom

fig. 48

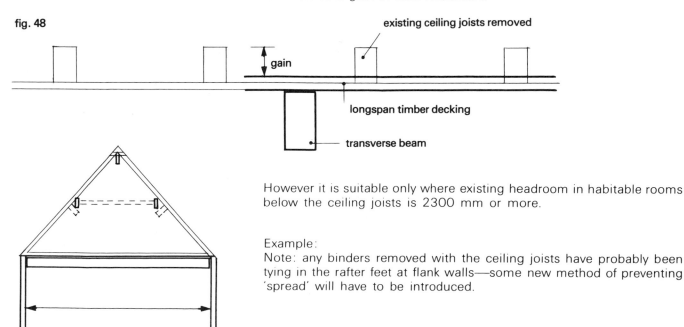

existing ceiling joists removed

gain

longspan timber decking

transverse beam

However it is suitable only where existing headroom in habitable rooms below the ceiling joists is 2300 mm or more.

Example:
Note: any binders removed with the ceiling joists have probably been tying in the rafter feet at flank walls—some new method of preventing 'spread' will have to be introduced.

53

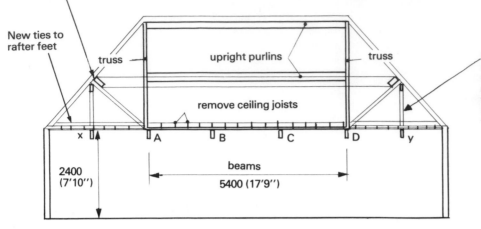

existing angle purlin can remain across hip

New ties to rafter feet

truss

upright purlins

remove ceiling joists

truss

posts, supported by beams (x to y) (or a truss could be used) to carry a new purlin set vertically. This purlin will remove a large proportion of the horizontal 'spread' forces at flank wall.

x   A   B   C   D   y

2400 (7'10")

beams
5400 (17'9")

fig. 49

Long span timber decking (see table on p46 'continuous span'):
38 mm redwood/whitewood 50 grade can span 1870 mm (6 ft 1½ in)
5400 total floorlength required = 3 spans x 1800 mm

Beams B and C
Assume total loading of 175 kg/m² ∴total load on each beam B and C is 1.8 x 5 x 175 = 1575 kg. 5 m beam. ∴load per m run = 315 kg
Assume beam width of 100 mm (10 cm) ∴unit distributed load = 31.5 kg/m/cm. From 'Span charts for solid timber' (TRADA publication) with no load sharing and long term loading;
100 x 275 mm keruing 65 grade, air dry
or
2 x 50 x 275 mm keruing 65 grade, air dry together at 600 mm centres

Beams A and D
Total load on each beam is 1.8 x 5 x 175 = 787.5 kg. Unit distributed load is ½ that for beam B or C. ∴the beam width can be halved: 50 x 275 mm keruing 65 grade, air dry.

Headroom below beam: existing ceiling height 2400 − 275 beam = 2125 mm satisfactory (2000 mm permitted minimum).

Trussed and plybox beams (suitable for combined purlin/floor beam)
As the depth of a beam increases, the bending stresses at top and bottom decrease and so less material is required thus reducing the weight. There are various methods of achieving this using small section timbers and plywood:

i   Plywoodweb I beam

fig. 50

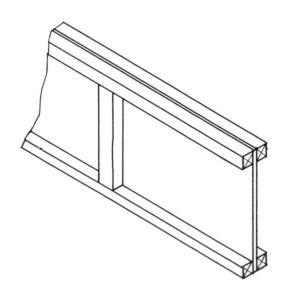

ii Diagonal boarding box beam

fig. 51

iii 'Sandwich' trussed beam

fig. 52

iv Trussed beam

fig. 53

v Plybox beam

fig. 54

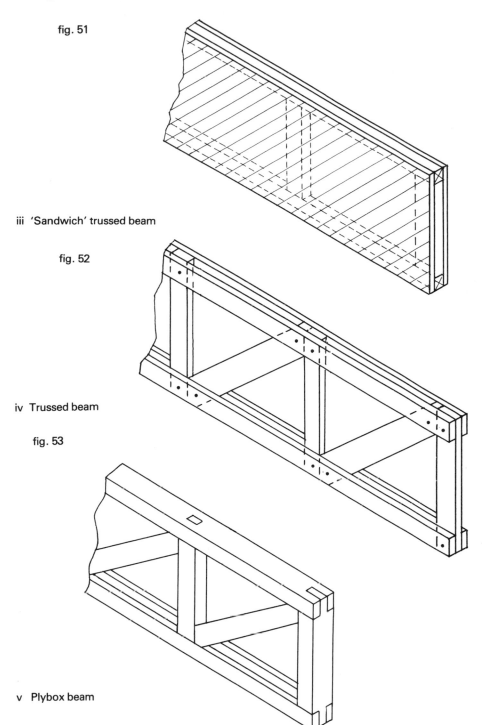

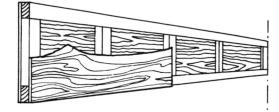

of these
i glued construction with pressure from clamps or nails (factory process, warm, dry atmosphere is essential)
ii the web may be single as in i
iii requires either bolted connections at every joint (expensive) or pressure jointing with double-sided truss plates
iv requires skilled traditional jointing techniques (expensive) or butt jointed with truss plates (factory process)

v can be constructed using close-nailing and is therefore the most suitable for attic 'workshop' methods.

NB Where truss plates are mentioned, nailed (or glued) plywood gussets can be used.

If radical alterations to the roof are being done, it may be possible to make the beam off site and lift it into place. However, where this is not possible the plybox beam can be made on the attic floor and easily tilted into position due to its light weight. Its length will be slightly less than the attic length, using metal joist hangers as described on p 47.

The beam is made from plywood sheets nailed at close centres to softwood battens. Joints between sheets in the length of the beam must be backed by plywood splicing gussets. Refer to the TRADA publication 'Introduction to the design of plyweb beams' E/1B/24.

The total loads carried by the beam = purlin load (roof deadload + imposed load) + (floorbeam load + imposed load) + floorbeam load (floor deadload + imposed load).

SIZE OF RAFTERS

Deadload on rafters between 50 and 75 kg/m² measured on slope. From Schedule 6 (roofslope 30° to 42½°). N.B. The maximum span tables given in Schedule 6 now refer only to stress graded timber to BS 4978.

fig. 55

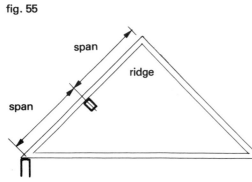

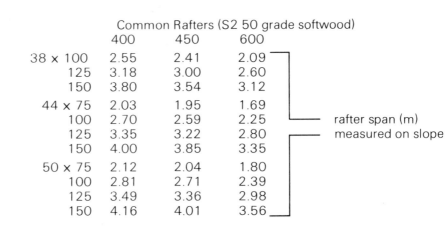

Common Rafters (S2 50 grade softwood)			
	400	450	600
38 x 100	2.55	2.41	2.09
125	3.18	3.00	2.60
150	3.80	3.54	3.12
44 x 75	2.03	1.95	1.69
100	2.70	2.59	2.25
125	3.35	3.22	2.80
150	4.00	3.85	3.35
50 x 75	2.12	2.04	1.80
100	2.81	2.71	2.39
125	3.49	3.36	2.98
150	4.16	4.01	3.56

rafter span (m) measured on slope

TO CHECK SIZE OF EXISTING PURLIN OR TO CALCULATE SIZE OF NEW SOLID PURLIN

1 Calculate total load on each 1 m run of purlin (see pp 58-59)
2 Required purlin span? Effective span can be reduced by strutting off walls.

fig. 56

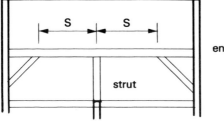

3 Select a width of purlin and divide load/m run by the width to give the unit distributed load in kg/m run/cm width (refer to table on p43,which gives sizes for keruing 65 grade hardwood for certain spans and certain unit distribution loads — ignore the column headings 'width of floor/m, 1, 1.5, 2 m etc'. For other values, spans and timbers, refer to 'Span tables for domestic purlin' (TRADA publication E/1B/14 Jan 1970) and to table 12 schedule 6 purlins (S2 50 grade softwood) supporting rafters to which table 11 relates.

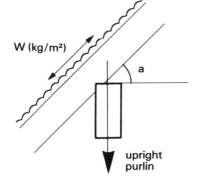

fig. 57

W (kg/m²)

a

upright
purlin

Calculation of loading on purlin
DEADLOAD
The deadload (measured on slope) from the roof tiles, battens, felt, rafters, insulation etc when resolved, produces a vertical or plan

$$\text{load} = \frac{W}{\text{Cos } a°}$$

Weights of various roofing materials are shown in the table below with their equivalent vertical loads for roof pitches 30°, 35°, 40°, 45°, and 50°

DEADLOADS ON PITCHED ROOF

A

a°

B

	A Actual weight of materials kg/m²	B Equivalent load measured on plan kg/m²				
a° cos a° mm		30° 0.8660	35° 0.8192	40° 0.7660	45° 0.7071	50° 0.6428
Concrete plain tiles	66.0	76.21	80.56	86.16	93.34	102.67
interlocking	50.0	57.74	61.03	65.27	70.71	77.78
Clay plain tiles	65.0	75.05	79.34	84.85	91.92	101.12
'Hardrow' concrete slates 14	80.0	92.38	97.65	104.44	113.14	124.45
Natural slates	50.0	57.74	61.03	65.27	70.71	77.78
Asbestos/cement 6	28.0	32.33	34.18	36.55	39.60	43.55
slates 4	20.0	23.10	24.41	26.11	28.28	31.11
Asbestos/cement diagonal 4	13.0	15.01	15.87	16.97	18.38	20.22
3 layer bituminous felt	9.0	10.40	11.00	11.80	12.60	14.00
battens and underslating felt	4.0	4.62	4.88	5.22	5.66	6.22
Rafters (average)	14.0	16.16	17.09	18.27	19.80	21.78
Insulating quilt 25	1.0	1.15	1.22	1.30	1.40	1.55
50	2.0	2.30	2.44	2.60	2.80	3.10
Plasterboard 9.5	8.5	9.81	10.37	11.10	12.02	13.22
12.7	11.0	12.70	13.42	14.36	15.55	17.11
19.0	17.0	19.63	20.75	22.19	24.04	26.45
Softwood boarding 21.0	11.0	12.70	13.42	14.36	15.55	17.11
Plywood 9.5	5.0	5.77	6.10	6.53	7.07	7.78
12.7	7.0	8.10	8.54	9.14	9.89	10.89
Fibre insulating board 9.5	2.5	2.88	3.05	3.26	3.53	3.89
12.7	3.5	4.04	4.27	4.57	4.95	5.44
19.0	5.0	5.77	6.10	6.53	7.07	7.78

IMPOSED LOAD:
A combination of snow load and maintenance/repair access load, totalling 720 N/m² (73.4 kg/m²) area measured on plan.
This value is reduced by 50 N (5.1 kg) for every 3° by which the pitch exceeds 30° (ie by 8.5 kg for every 5°):
30° — 73.4 kg/m²
35° — 64.9 kg/m²
40° — 56.4 kg/m²
45° — 47.9 kg/m²
50° — 39.4 kg/m²
Fixing between new purlin and existing rafters is best done by multigrip metal framing-anchors described previously.
'Birdsmouthing' of existing rafters is not recommended.

CALCULATION OF TOTAL LOADING ON 1M RUN OF EACH PURLIN/FLOOR BEAM

A 2 Purlin roof

a FROM ROOF: (Deadload* + imposed load) $\times (\frac{A}{2} + \frac{B}{2})$

b FROM FLOOR: (Total floorload $\times \frac{A}{2}$) + ($\frac{B}{2} \times$ deadweight only of ceiling)

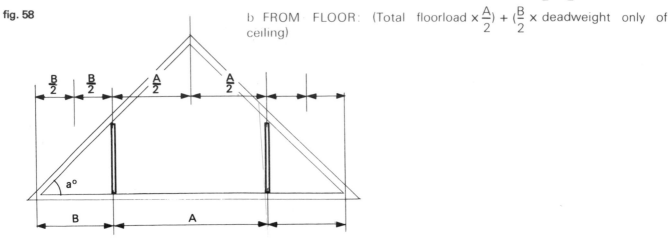

fig. 58

Total load on each purlin/beam = a + b

B 3 Purlin roof

RIDGE PURLIN: Roofload only = (deadload* + imposed load) $\times \frac{A}{2}$

PURLIN/FLOOR BEAM:

a From roof: (deadload* + imposed load) $\times (\frac{A}{4} + \frac{B}{2})$

b From floor: (total floor load $\times \frac{A}{2}$) + ($\frac{B}{2} \times$ deadweight only of ceiling)

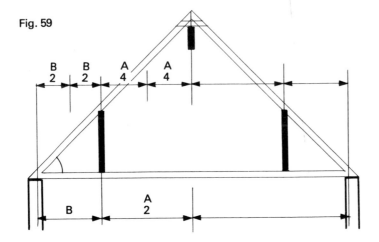

Fig. 59

Addition of the ridge purlin in B helps in reducing the load carried on the two purlin/floor beams and thus may be of use in some situations (eg where the roof covering is very heavy, or where the span is large). Note that headroom in a habitable room under the ridge purlin must be not less than 2000 mm (6 ft 7 in) providing the ceiling is not less than 2300 mm.

C 4 Purlin roof

Suitable for dormer window construction (upper purlin acts as a trimmer for the rafters above).

Roofload on each of the 2 upper purlins = (deadload* + imposed load) $\times (\frac{D + C}{2})$

Roofload on each of the 2 lower purlins = (deadload* + imposed load) $\times (\frac{C}{2} + \frac{B}{2})$

*measured on plan, see page 57.

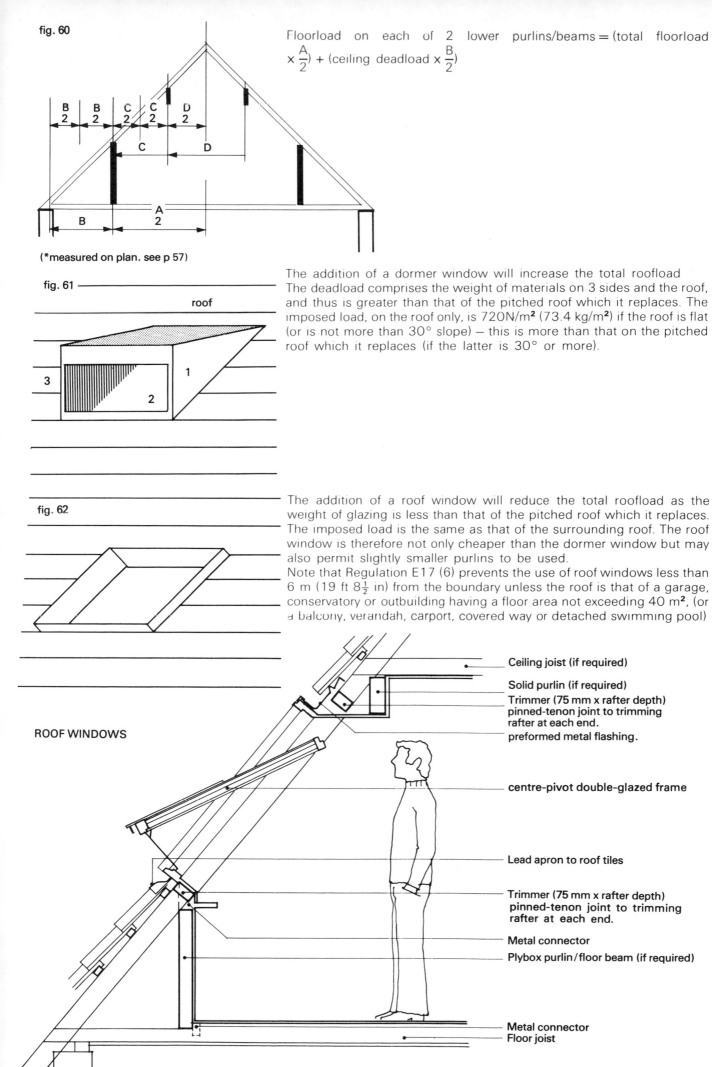

fig. 60

Floorload on each of 2 lower purlins/beams = (total floorload $\times \frac{A}{2}$) + (ceiling deadload $\times \frac{B}{2}$)

(*measured on plan. see p 57)

fig. 61 —————

roof

fig. 62

ROOF WINDOWS

The addition of a dormer window will increase the total roofload
The deadload comprises the weight of materials on 3 sides and the roof, and thus is greater than that of the pitched roof which it replaces. The imposed load, on the roof only, is 720N/m² (73.4 kg/m²) if the roof is flat (or is not more than 30° slope) — this is more than that on the pitched roof which it replaces (if the latter is 30° or more).

The addition of a roof window will reduce the total roofload as the weight of glazing is less than that of the pitched roof which it replaces. The imposed load is the same as that of the surrounding roof. The roof window is therefore not only cheaper than the dormer window but may also permit slightly smaller purlins to be used.
Note that Regulation E17 (6) prevents the use of roof windows less than 6 m (19 ft 8½ in) from the boundary unless the roof is that of a garage, conservatory or outbuilding having a floor area not exceeding 40 m², (or a balcony, verandah, carport, covered way or detached swimming pool)

Ceiling joist (if required)

Solid purlin (if required)

Trimmer (75 mm x rafter depth) pinned-tenon joint to trimming rafter at each end.

preformed metal flashing.

centre-pivot double-glazed frame

Lead apron to roof tiles

Trimmer (75 mm x rafter depth) pinned-tenon joint to trimming rafter at each end.

Metal connector

Plybox purlin/floor beam (if required)

Metal connector
Floor joist

Typical section through roof window

Typical section through roof window

Manufacturer	Type	Notes	Roof slope
'Velux' The Velux Co Ltd (Sales) Gunnels Wood Rd, Stevenage, Herts. SG1 2BN (Factory) Telford Road, Eastfield Indus. Estate, Glenrothes, Fife. 6 stock sizes in each type: 550×700, 780×980, 1340×980, 1140×1180, 780×1400, 1340×1380 (W×H)	fva	Clear-finish softwood frame, centre pivot, aluminium external cladding. Coupled sash for glazing on site.	30°–70°
	fvg	As type 'fva' but factory-glazed with clear sheet glass.	30°–70°
	ggl	A more advanced type. Single sash in clear-finish softwood, aluminium external cladding, sealed double-glazed unit fitted in factory, ventilator along top. Weight of 6 stock sizes: From 17 kg to 52 kg.	20°–85°
E L HIRZ KG UK Distributors Sewell & Sewell 86 Wellmeadow Road, Catford, London	fe standard roof window	Impregnated softwood with stainless steel cladding. Centre pivot. 5 sizes: 550×700, 780×980, 1140×1180, 1340×980, 1340×1400.	20°–70°
	'wingopan' attic	Zinc coated steel, painted, in stained softwood. Factory-glazed (double-glazed). Can be opened completely for escape. 8 sizes: 700×1030, 700×1350, 900×1350, 900×1550, 1300×1350, 1300×1550, 1500×1350, 1500×1750, 1300×1550, 1500×1350, 1500×1750. Weights: 28 to 81 kg.	18°–85°
	'Euroluc' steel skylight	Low cost galv. steel tophung. Puttyless glazing with 5 mm acrylic sheet.	From $17\frac{1}{2}°$

Note: The inclusion of a trade name does not imply approval of that product by TRADA, nor does omission imply disapproval.

	Thickness mm	Structure (3) Weight kg/m²
softwood boarding	19	9.1
	22	11.0
	25	1.0
plywood Douglas fir	12.5	6.7
British made	12.5	7.8
Finnish birch	12.5	8.7
European beech	12.5	9.3
blockboard	25	10.2
wood chipboard	12.5	9.6
	19	14.6
	22	16.1
low density extruded	50	9.0
hardboard	3.2	3.0 to 3.3
(weight varies according	4.8	4.3 to 4.8
to brand)	6.4	5.7 to 6.6
medium board	6	4.4 to 4.6
(weight varies according	9	6.3 to 6.8
to brand)	12	7.3 to 8.9
fibre insulation board	9.5	2.5 to 2.7
(weight varies according	12.7	3.2 to 3.7
to brand)	19	4.4 to 5.4
	25	6.4 to 7.6
gypsum plasterboard	9.5	8.5
	12.5	11.2
	19	17.1
corkboard	25	4.9
woodwool slab	25	14.6
asbestos insulation board	6.4	4.6
	9.5	6.7
	12.7	9.2
mineral-wool quilt	25	3.4
	50	6.8
insulating felt	25	4.9
plaster lightweight (2 coat)	10	10
gypsum (2 coat)	13	23.4

Floors section

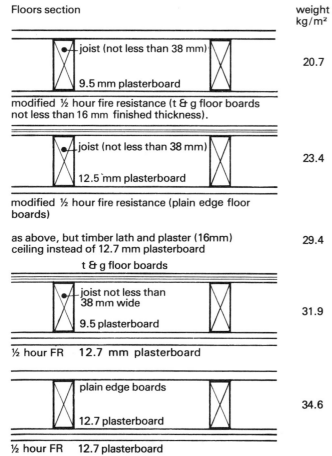

weight kg/m²

joist (not less than 38 mm)
9.5 mm plasterboard — 20.7
modified ½ hour fire resistance (t & g floor boards not less than 16 mm finished thickness).

joist (not less than 38 mm)
12.5 mm plasterboard — 23.4
modified ½ hour fire resistance (plain edge floor boards)

as above, but timber lath and plaster (16mm) ceiling instead of 12.7 mm plasterboard — 29.4

t & g floor boards
joist not less than 38 mm wide
9.5 plasterboard — 31.9
½ hour FR   12.7 mm plasterboard

plain edge boards
12.7 plasterboard — 34.6
½ hour FR   12.7 plasterboard

Partitions plan

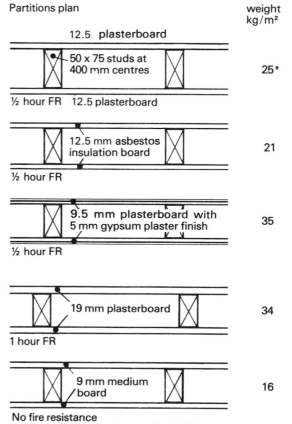

weight kg/m²

12.5 plasterboard
50 x 75 studs at 400 mm centres — 25*
½ hour FR   12.5 plasterboard

12.5 mm asbestos insulation board — 21
½ hour FR

9.5 mm plasterboard with 5 mm gypsum plaster finish — 35
½ hour FR

19 mm plasterboard — 34
1 hour FR

9 mm medium board — 16
No fire resistance (weight of studs taken as 3 kg/m²)

*load bearing

Stairs

7

THE BUILDING REGULATIONS 1976

— applies (in the context of these Guides) to a new stair put into an existing house (eg up to an attic converted into a bedroom) or put into a new extension built onto an existing house.

Part H — does not apply to an existing stair which will remain unaffected by any alterations to the house. However, the building inspector may require a new stair to be put in if the existing stair is structurally unsafe, in which case Part H will apply.

Part H could apply to an existing stair if alterations to the house adversely affect the stair (eg by reducing headroom over the stair so that it contravenes the headroom requirements in Part H more than it did before). Another example is the raising of floor levels, by laying a screed on the ground floor or a 'floating floor' on the upper floor, which results in unequal rises at top and bottom. This contravenes Part H, and the building inspector could order the stair to be rebuilt.

The local authority may permit a relaxation of Part H in some cases. Part H is summarised, with examples, in this leaflet. Tables of dimensions, for the steepest stairs permitted, are included. The steepest stair takes up the least area on plan and uses the least material in its construction. It is therefore usually the cheapest.

Part H classifies domestic stairs under 2 headings:

Private stair

serving a one-family dwelling (eg 1 house or 1 maisonette). The steepest angle permitted is 42°

Common stair

serving more than one dwelling (eg to 2 or more flats or maisonettes). The steepest angle permitted is 38°

Design procedure

1 Measure the floor to floor height: this is the total rise (R) of the proposed stair.

2 'Private' or 'Common' stair? (Serving one family or more than one family?)

3 How much floor area is available on plan? — It is most economical (in cost and use of floor area) to put in the steepest stair permitted: 42° or 38°

4 Private stair: If 42° stair angle is used, the dimensions of 'going', 'rise' and 'pitch line' can be read directly off the table on p66. The number of equal rises required for the total rise can be read directly off the table on p67, and the total going determined.

If an angle less than 42° is chosen, calculate the number of equal rises required: each rise to be not more than 220 mm, the going = the rise ÷ tangent (stair angle)° (not less than 220 mm).

5 Common stair: If 38° stair angle is used, refer to the tables on p73 and p 74.

If an angle less than 38° is chosen, calculate the number of equal rises required:

each rise to be not more than 190 mm, the going = the rise ÷ tangent (stair angle)° (not less than 230 mm).

6 Decide on the plan form:

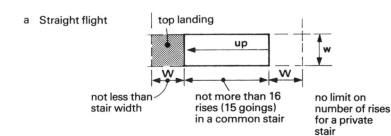

a   Straight flight

top landing

up

w

not less than stair width

not more than 16 rises (15 goings) in a common stair

no limit on number of rises for a private stair

b Two flight ½ turn

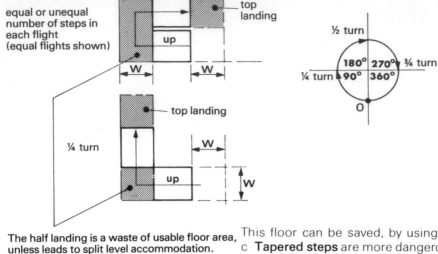

equal or unequal
number of steps in
each flight
(equal flights shown)

top landing

up

W W

½ turn

¼ turn ¾ turn

180° 270°

¼ turn 90° 360°

O

¼ turn

top landing

W

up

W

The half landing is a waste of usable floor area, unless leads to split level accommodation.

This floor can be saved, by using tapered steps as follows:

c Tapered steps are more dangerous than parallel steps, but can be used (subject to the limitations shown on pages 68, 69 and 74). The following stair plans are possible:

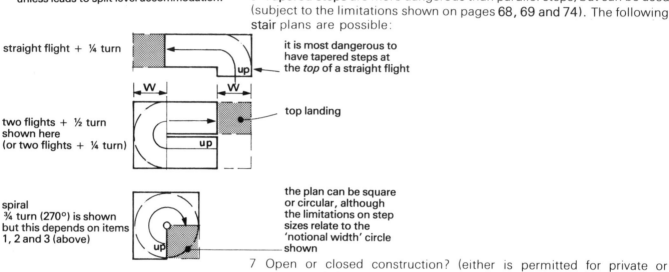

straight flight + ¼ turn

it is most dangerous to
have tapered steps at
the *top* of a straight flight

up

W W

two flights + ½ turn
shown here
(or two flights + ¼ turn)

top landing

up

spiral
¾ turn (270°) is shown
but this depends on items
1, 2 and 3 (above)

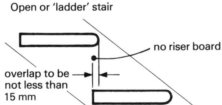

the plan can be square
or circular, although
the limitations on step
sizes relate to the
'notional width' circle
shown

up

7 Open or closed construction? (either is permitted for private or common stairs)

Open or 'ladder' stair

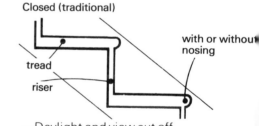

no riser board

overlap to be
not less than
15 mm

Closed (traditional)

with or without
nosing

tread

riser

Daylight — The main advantage is that daylight and view is not totally cut off by the stair.

Separation — Cannot be used to separate one room from another.

Finishes — Difficult to carpet.

Safety — Dangerous for small children.

Storage — Space below cannot be used for concealed storage.

Making — Simple construction but the lack of risers reduces the stair stiffness: therefore thicker treads have to be used.

Material — Exposed treads are usually of hardwood for appearance and strength. A thickness of not less than 38 mm is recommended.

Construction — The treads are usually housed in a 13 mm deep trench in the stringer and fixed with dowels through the stringer. Alternatively, metal brackets or timber ledger supports are used but these are seen from below.

— Daylight and view cut off.

— Can be used to separate one room from another.

— Easy to carpet.

— Not dangerous.

— Space below can provide concealed storage.

— Fairly complicated construction but economical due to the use of standard stair machines in joinery workshops.

— Tread thickness is usually 21 mm and riser thickness is usually 14 mm, both softwood.

— The treads and risers are usually housed in 13 mm deep trenches in the stringer and wedged and glued from below. Triangular blocks are glued between the treads and risers.

— Both methods require stringers (side members) at least 225 mm deep to house the ends of the treads (and risers) completely. This depth is not required structurally in many cases.

It is cheaper to use a smaller-depth stringer, and allow the treads to project beyond the top of the stringer.

The drawings below show how a 150 mm deep stringer relates closely to the range of rise/going sizes for common stair 38° pitch (left) and private stair 42° pitch (right).

The thickness of the materials and any nosing projection or overlap of treads in an 'open' stair will, of course, project beyond the lines.

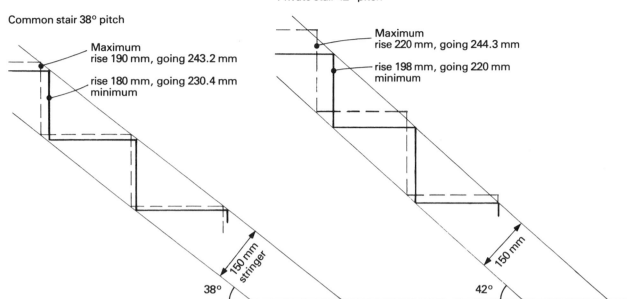

Private stair 42° pitch

Maximum
rise 220 mm, going 244.3 mm

rise 198 mm, going 220 mm
minimum

150 mm

42°

Common stair 38° pitch

Maximum
rise 190 mm, going 243.2 mm

rise 180 mm, going 230.4 mm
minimum

150 mm
stringer

38°

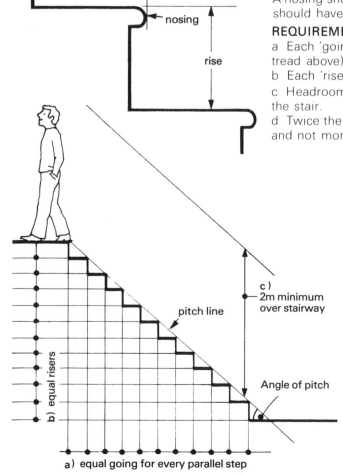

'going'

tread

nosing

rise

Regulations

Each step consists of a 'going' and a 'rise'. The 'going' is the same as the 'tread' when there is no projecting nosing. The nosing is not compulsory although open-riser stairs are required to have 15 mm overlap of the treads.

A nosing should not project more than 25 mm to avoid toe-catching and should have a rounded profile.

REQUIREMENTS FOR 'PRIVATE' AND 'COMMON' STAIRS:

a Each 'going' (which is the width of each tread less any overlap by the tread above) shall be equal.

b Each 'rise' shall be equal. This applies to landings as well as steps.

c Headroom above the stair shall be as shown, over the whole width of the stair.

d Twice the 'rise' + the 'going' (2r + g) should be not less than 550 mm and not more than 700 mm.

c)
2m minimum
over stairway

pitch line

Angle of pitch

b) equal risers

a) equal going for every parallel step

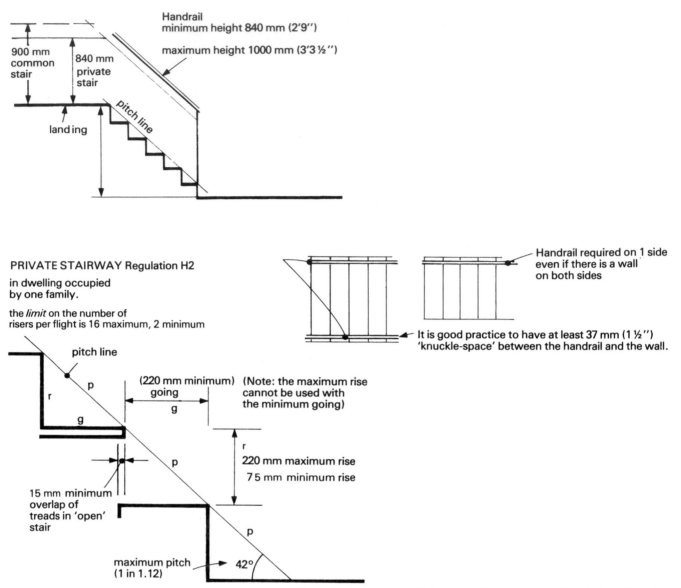

Handrail
minimum height 840 mm (2'9'')

maximum height 1000 mm (3'3½'')

900 mm common stair

840 mm private stair

landing

pitch line

PRIVATE STAIRWAY Regulation H2

in dwelling occupied by one family.

the *limit* on the number of risers per flight is 16 maximum, 2 minimum

pitch line

p

r

g

p

(220 mm minimum) going g

(Note: the maximum rise cannot be used with the minimum going)

r
220 mm maximum rise
75 mm minimum rise

15 mm minimum overlap of treads in 'open' stair

p

maximum pitch (1 in 1.12)

42°

Handrail required on 1 side even if there is a wall on both sides

It is good practice to have at least 37 mm (1½'') 'knuckle-space' between the handrail and the wall.

Permissible range of risers and goings for 42° 'private' stairs

Permissible range of risers and goings for 42° 'private' stair
All dimensions shown in millimetres (mm)

$$42° \qquad g = \frac{r}{\tan 42°} = \frac{r}{0.9004} \qquad p = \frac{r}{\sin 42°} = \frac{r}{0.6691}$$

rise r mm	going g mm	pitch g line mm	2 r+g	Total R rise	Total G going	Total P
220	244.3	328	684.3	3300	3420	4932
218	242.1	326	678.1	3270	3389	4887
216	239.9	323	671.9	3240	3358	4842
214	237.7	320	666.4	3210	3328	4797
212	235.5	317	659.5	3180	3297	4752
210	233.2	314	653.2	3150	3265	4708
208	231	311	647	3120	3234	4663
206	228.8	308	640.8	3090	3203	4618
204	226.6	305	634.6	3060	3172	4573
202	224.4	302	628.4	3030	3141	4528
200	222.2	299	622.2	3000	3311	4484
198	220	296	616.0	2970	3080	4439

Not less than 550 mm and not more than 700 mm

Example: stair with 15 rises and 14 goings. See page 6 for table of stairs from 5 r/4 g to 16 r/15 g

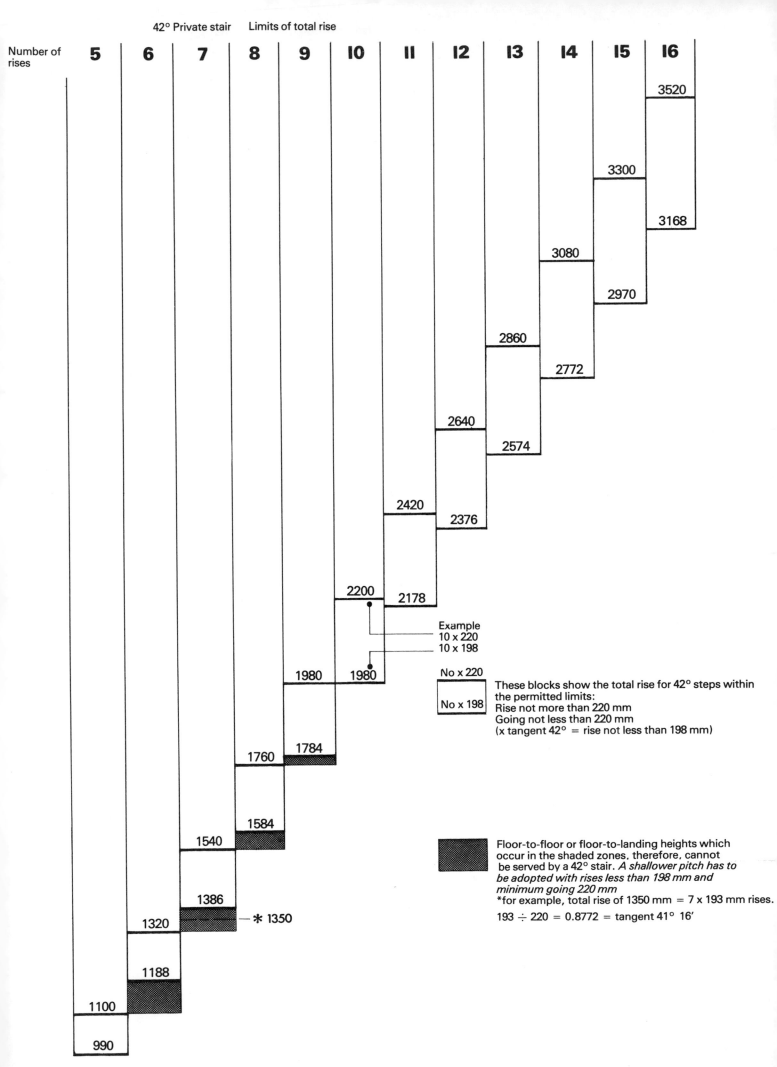

42° Private stair Limits of total rise

5 6 7 8 9 10 11 12 13 14 15 16

3520

3300

3168

3080

2970

2860

2772

2640

2574

2420

2376

2200 2178

Example
10 × 220
10 × 198

1980 1980

No × 220

These blocks show the total rise for 42° steps within the permitted limits:
Rise not more than 220 mm
Going not less than 220 mm
(x tangent 42° = rise not less than 198 mm)

No × 198

1760 1784

1584

1540

1386

1320 —✳ 1350

Floor-to-floor or floor-to-landing heights which occur in the shaded zones, therefore, cannot be served by a 42° stair. *A shallower pitch has to be adopted with rises less than 198 mm and minimum going 220 mm*
*for example, total rise of 1350 mm = 7 × 193 mm rises.

193 ÷ 220 = 0.8772 = tangent 41° 16'

1188

1100

990

Table of total rise and going for 42° stairs, with 5 to 16 rises, from 198 mm to 220 mm each rise

Rise r	Total rise R 5r	Total going G 4g	R 6r	G 5g	R 7r	G 6g	R 8r	G 7g	R 9r	G 8g	R 10r	G 9g
220	1100	977	1320	1221	1540	1466	1760	1710	1980	1954	2200	2199
218	1090	968	1308	1210	1526	1453	1744	1695	1962	1937	2180	2179
216	1080	959	1296	1199	1512	1439	1728	1679	1944	1919	2160	2159
214	1070	951	1284	1188	1498	1426	1712	1664	1926	1901	2140	2139
212	1060	942	1272	1177	1484	1413	1696	1648	1908	1884	2120	2119
210	1050	933	1260	1166	1470	1399	1680	1632	1890	1866	2100	2099
208	1040	924	1248	1155	1456	1386	1664	1617	1872	1848	2080	2079
206	1030	915	1236	1144	1442	1373	1648	1601	1854	1830	2060	2059
204	1020	906	1224	1133	1428	1360	1632	1586	1836	1813	2040	2039
202	1010	897	1212	1122	1414	1346	1616	1571	1818	1795	2020	2020
200	1000	888	1200	1111	1400	1333	1600	1555	1800	1777	2000	2000
198	990	880	1188	1100	1386	1320	1584	1540	1784	1760	1980	1980

r	11r	10g	12r	11g	13r	12g	14r	13g	15r	14g	16r	15g
220	2420	2443	2640	2687	2860	2932	3080	3176	3300	3420	3520	3664
218	2398	2421	2616	2663	2834	2905	3052	3147	3270	3389	3488	3631
216	2376	2399	2592	2639	2808	2879	3024	3118	3240	3359	3456	3598
214	2354	2377	2568	2615	2782	2852	2996	3090	3210	3328	3424	3565
212	2332	2355	2544	2590	2756	2826	2968	3061	3180	3297	3392	3532
210	2310	2332	2520	2565	2730	2798	2940	3032	3150	3265	3360	3498
208	2288	2310	2496	2541	2704	2772	2912	3003	3120	3234	3328	3465
206	2266	2288	2472	2517	2678	2746	2874	2974	3090	3203	3296	3432
204	2244	2266	2448	2493	2652	2719	2856	2946	3060	3172	3264	3399
202	2222	2244	2424	2468	2626	2693	2828	2917	3030	3142	3232	3366
200	2200	2222	2400	2444	2600	2666	2800	2888	3000	3111	3200	3333
198	2178	2200	2376	2420	2574	2640	2772	2860	2970	3080	3168	3300

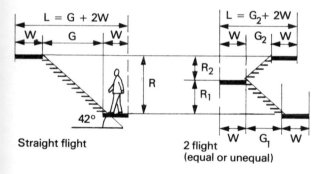

Straight flight

2 flight
(equal or unequal)

L = The total length required for stair and access

W = Access space at top and bottom of stair (should be not less than the width of the stair)

The half-landing takes the place of one going: the total number of goings in $G_1 + G_2$ is one less than G for a straight flight.

Tapered steps (a)

The requirements for (B) equal rises (C) headroom and handrails (see page 65) apply to tapered steps. The rise (r) must be not more than 220 mm.

line of notional width (headroom required within it)

actual tread length can exceed the notional width, but the width of top and bottom tapered steps must be equal to each other and to adjacent parallel steps.

PRIVATE STAIR

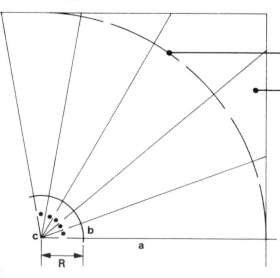

The limitations are:
a the width is not less than 800 mm
b the going is not less than 75 mm
c All angles of taper in
a stair should be equal.
The minimum radius R when
b = 75 and c = 20° is 216 mm.
R can be less than this if c is more than 20°

$(R = \dfrac{75}{2}$ mm $\div \sin \dfrac{C}{2})$. Example: $C = 22\frac{1}{2}°$ $\dfrac{\sin 22\frac{1}{2}°}{2} = 0.1951$

$\therefore R = \dfrac{37.5}{0.1951} = 192$ mm

Spiral stair

The overall diameter D of a spiral stair = 2(R + a)
The steepest spiral stair permitted has R = 216 mm. When C = 20°
The minimum D for these values is 2(216 + 750) = 1932 mm. 750 mm is too narrow to carry furniture — 850 mm is preferred $\therefore$ D = 2(216 + 850) = 2132 mm. The following examples assume the maximum permitted rise of 220 mm. Refer to the table on page 68 for the total rise/number of rises for different rises (not exceeding 220 mm).

Examples 1 to 4

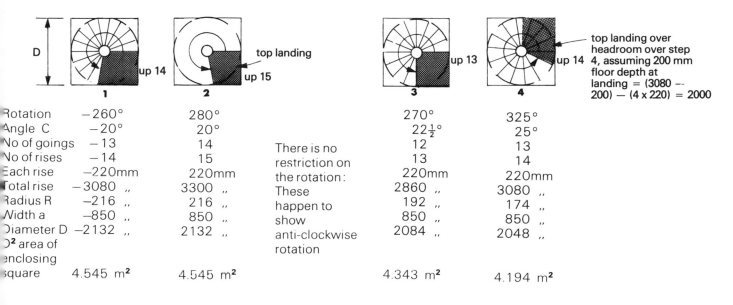

top landing over headroom over step 4, assuming 200 mm floor depth at landing = (3080 − 200) − (4 x 220) = 2000

	1	2		3	4
Rotation	−260°	280°		270°	325°
Angle C	−20°	20°		22½°	25°
No of goings	−13	14	There is no	12	13
No of rises	−14	15	restriction on	13	14
Each rise	−220mm	220mm	the rotation:	220mm	220mm
Total rise	−3080 „	3300 „	These	2860 „	3080 „
Radius R	−216 „	216 „	happen to	192 „	174 „
Width a	−850 „	850 „	show	850 „	850 „
Diameter D	−2132 „	2132 „	anti-clockwise	2084 „	2048 „
D² area of enclosing square	4.545 m²	4.545 m²	rotation	4.343 m²	4.194 m²

Note: As angle C increases so the values of D and D² reduce. Compare 1 and 4 which have the same total rise etc but different angle C values. However, 25° appears to be the limit — due to headroom below the top landing: example 4* is just adequate but any reduction in the rise below 220 mm would make the headroom inadequate.

Comparison of different plan-forms assuming total rise = 2860 mm = 13 rises × 220 mm.
Pitch of parallel steps = 42°. W = 850 mm.

Plan (not to scale)	Stair type	Overall length incl. top & bottom landings	Area of rectangle over all stair landings	Comments
5 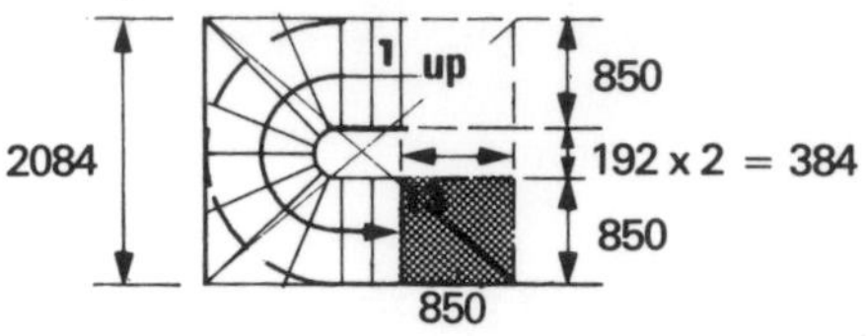 2084, 850, 192 × 2 = 384, 850, 850	**Tapered steps** 180° rotation 22½° angle of taper	2,381 mm	4.962 m²	This type has the shortest stair length, front to back. The corners outside the notional width can be used as pipe ducts etc.
6 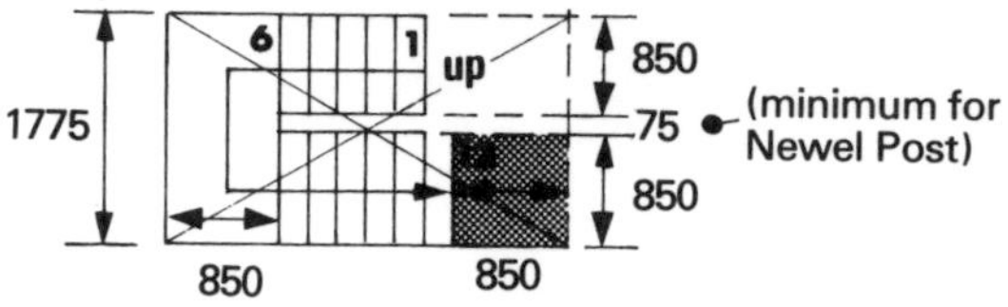 1775, 850, 75 (minimum for Newel Post), 850, 850, 850	**Two flight** ½ turn	3,166	5.619	Introduction of tapered steps instead of the half-landing would result in plan 5: the central well between has to be increased. Largest area of the four alternatives shown here.
7 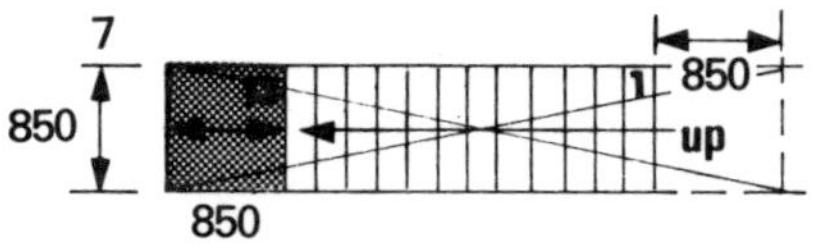 850, 850, 850	**Straight flight**	5,482	4.659	The longest of those shown here, but requires the least plan width.
8 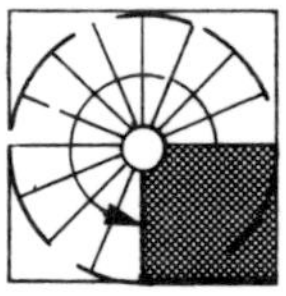	**Spiral** 270° turn	2,084	4.343	The smallest floor area. Top landing directly over bottom landing.

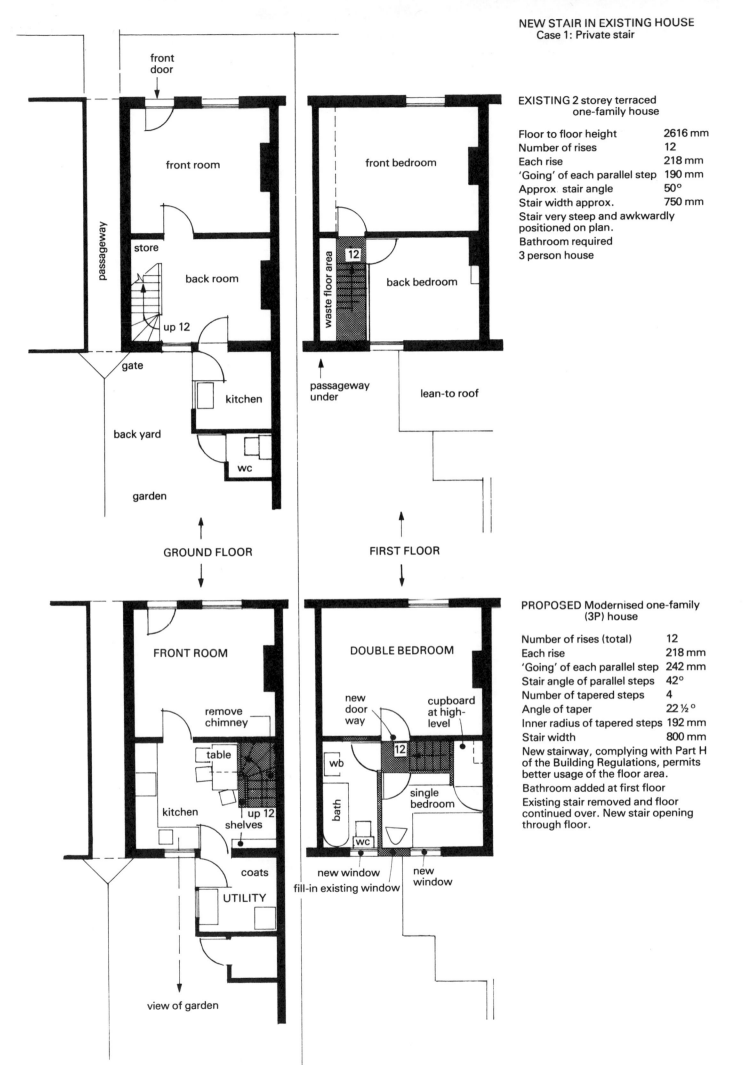

GROUND FLOOR (existing)

- front door
- front room
- passageway
- store
- back room
- up 12
- gate
- kitchen
- back yard
- wc
- garden

FIRST FLOOR (existing)

- front bedroom
- waste floor area
- 12
- back bedroom
- passageway under
- lean-to roof

EXISTING 2 storey terraced one-family house

Floor to floor height	2616 mm
Number of rises	12
Each rise	218 mm
'Going' of each parallel step	190 mm
Approx. stair angle	50°
Stair width approx.	750 mm

Stair very steep and awkwardly positioned on plan.
Bathroom required
3 person house

GROUND FLOOR (proposed)

- FRONT ROOM
- remove chimney
- table
- kitchen
- up 12
- shelves
- coats
- UTILITY
- view of garden

FIRST FLOOR (proposed)

- DOUBLE BEDROOM
- new door way
- cupboard at high-level
- 12
- wb
- bath
- single bedroom
- wc
- new window
- fill-in existing window
- new window

PROPOSED Modernised one-family (3P) house

Number of rises (total)	12
Each rise	218 mm
'Going' of each parallel step	242 mm
Stair angle of parallel steps	42°
Number of tapered steps	4
Angle of taper	22 ½ °
Inner radius of tapered steps	192 mm
Stair width	800 mm

New stairway, complying with Part H of the Building Regulations, permits better usage of the floor area.
Bathroom added at first floor
Existing stair removed and floor continued over. New stair opening through floor.

Case 2 : private stair

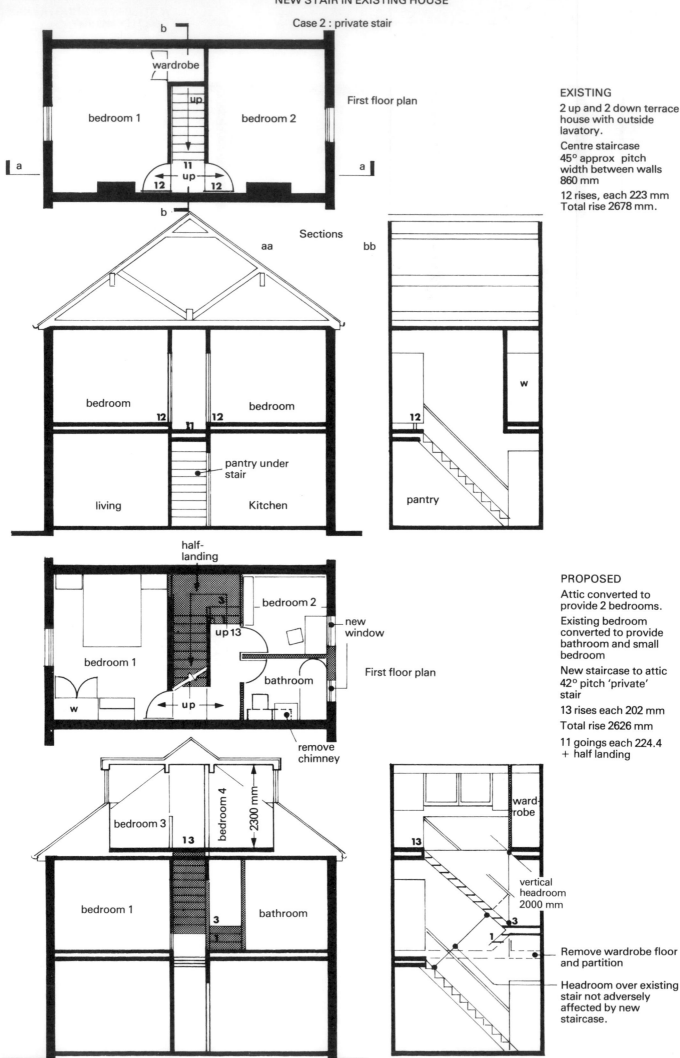

First floor plan

EXISTING

2 up and 2 down terrace house with outside lavatory.

Centre staircase 45° approx pitch width between walls 860 mm

12 rises, each 223 mm Total rise 2678 mm.

Sections aa   bb

bedroom   12   12   bedroom

living   pantry under stair   Kitchen

pantry   w   12

half-landing

bedroom 1   3   bedroom 2   up13   new window   bathroom   First floor plan

w   up

remove chimney

PROPOSED

Attic converted to provide 2 bedrooms.

Existing bedroom converted to provide bathroom and small bedroom

New staircase to attic 42° pitch 'private' stair

13 rises each 202 mm

Total rise 2626 mm

11 goings each 224.4 + half landing

bedroom 3   bedroom 4   2300 mm   13

bedroom 1   13   3   bathroom

ward-robe   13   3   1

vertical headroom 2000 mm

Remove wardrobe floor and partition

Headroom over existing stair not adversely affected by new staircase.

COMMON STAIRWAY
Regulation H3 (table)
In buildings occupied by more than one family (e g flats)
Not more than 16 risers/flight and not less than 2 risers/flight

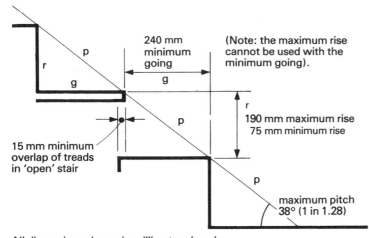

240 mm minimum going

(Note: the maximum rise cannot be used with the minimum going).

190 mm maximum rise
75 mm minimum rise

15 mm minimum overlap of treads in 'open' stair

maximum pitch 38° (1 in 1.28)

All dimensions shown in millimetres (mm)
Permissible range or rises and goings for 38° 'common' stair

$$38° \quad g = \frac{r}{\tan 38°} = \frac{r}{0.7812} \qquad p = \frac{r}{\sin 38°} = \frac{r}{0.6156}$$

Permissible range of rises and goings for 38° 'common' stair

rise r mm	going g mm	pitch p line mm	2r+g	Total R rise	Total G going	Total P
190	243.2	308.6	623.2	2850	3404.8	4629.6
189	241.9	307.0	619.9	2835	3386.6	4605.2
188	240.6	305.4	616.6	2820	3368.4	4580.9
187		303.7	613.3	2805	3350.9	4556.6
186		302.1	610.1	2790	3333.4	4532.2
185		300.5	606.8	2775	3313.7	4507.8
184		298.9	603.5	2760	3297.0	4483.4
183		297.3	600.2	2745	3279.8	4459.0
182		295.6	596.9	2730	3260.6	4434.6
181		294.0	593.6	2715	3243.1	4410.2
180		292.4	590.4	2700	3225.6	4386.0

Not less than 550 mm and not more than 700 mm

Example: stair with 15 rises and 14 goings. See below and next page for table of stairs from 5r/4g to 16r/15g.

Table of total rise and going for 38° stairs, 5 to 16 rises, 180 to 190 mm each rise.

Rise r	Total rise R 5r	Total going G 4g	R 6r	G 5g	R 7r	G 6g	R 8r	G 7g	R 9r	G 8g	R 10r	G 9g
190	950	973	1140	1216	1330	1459	1520	1702	1710	1946	1900	2189
189	945	968	1134	1209	1323	1451	1512	1693	1701	1935	1890	2177
188	940	962	1128	1203	1316	1444	1504	1684	1692	1925	1880	2165
187	935	957	1122	1196	1309	1436	1496	1675	1683	1914	1870	2154
186	930	952	1116	1190	1302	1429	1488	1667	1674	1905	1860	2143
185	925	947	1110	1184	1295	1421	1480	1658	1665	1894	1850	2131
184	920	942	1104	1177	1288	1413	1472	1648	1656	1884	1840	2119
183	915	937	1098	1171	1281	1405	1464	1639	1647	1874	1830	2108
182	910	932	1092	1164	1274	1397	1456	1630	1638	1863	1820	2096
181	905	927	1086	1158	1267	1390	1448	1621	1629	1853	1810	2084
180	900	922	1080	1152	1260	1382	1440	1613	1620	1843	1800	2074

Rise r	11r	10g	12r	11g	13r	12g	14r	13g	15r	14g	16r	15g
190	2090	2432	2280	2675	2470	2918	2660	3162	2850	3405	3040*	3648
189	2079	2419	2268	2661	2457	2903	2646	3145	2835	3387	3024	3628
188	2068	2406	2256	2647	2444	2887	2632	3128	2820	3368	3008	3609
187	2057	2393	2244	2632	2431	2872	2618	3111	2805	3350	2992	3589
186	2046	2381	2232	2619	2418	2857	2604	3095	2790	3333	2976	3571
185	2035	2368	2220	2605	2405	2841	2590	3078	2775	3315	2960	3552
184	2024	2355	2208	2590	2392	2826	2576	3061	2760	3297	2944	3532
183	2013	2342	2196	2576	2379	2810	2562	3045	2745	3279	2928	3513
182	2002	2329	2184	2562	2366	2795	2548	3028	2730	3261	2912	3493
181	1991	2316	2172	2548	2353	2779	2534	3011	2700	3242	2896	3474
180	1980	2304	2160	2534	2340	2765	2520	2995	2700	3226	2880	3456

*The maximum permitted for a single flight common stair

In a straight flight the number of 'goings' is one less than the number of 'rises' (as shown in the table above). In a 2 flight stair the number of 'goings' is two less than the number of 'rises', due to the half-landing.

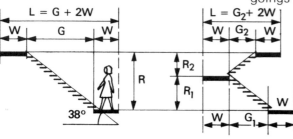

STRAIGHT FLIGHT   **2 FLIGHT**

L = the total length required for stair and access

W = access space at top and bottom of stair (should be not less than the stair width)

unequal flights shown here (headroom over lower flight critical) where flights are equal, then $G_1 = G_2$ and $R_1 = R_2$

Domestic stair design
tapered steps (b)

Common stair Some of the requirements for parallel steps apply to tapered steps: (B) (equal rises between consecutive floors); (C) (headroom); handrails (see page 65).

The requirements for 'goings' and stair angle are described below. There are simplified rules for private stairs between 750 and 1000 mm wide (page 69). The requirements on this page can be applied to private stairs, as an alternative method.

The Requirements:	'Common'	'Private'	Example:
g_2 shall be not less than	240 mm	220 mm	The steepest common stair permitted:
The pitch (stair angle) at g_2 shall be not more than	38°	42°	$g_2 = 240$, pitch 38° ∴ r = 240 × tan. 38° 185 mm.
The riser shall be not more than	190 mm	220 mm	so 185 mm is the maximum rise permitted
$2r + g_2$ shall be not less than	550 mm	550 mm	if the minimum going 240 mm is used at g_2.
$2r + g_3$ shall be not more than	700 mm	700 mm	Check: $2r + g_2 =$ 360 + 240 = 600 OK — more than 550.

Line of notional width. Headroom required within the notional width only.

Actual tread length can exceed the notional width: there is no outer limit but the width of top and bottom tapered steps must be equal to each other and to adjacent parallel steps.

The requirements for going and stair angle apply over the central zone, the width of which (W_1) is $W - (2 \times 270) = W - 540$ mm.

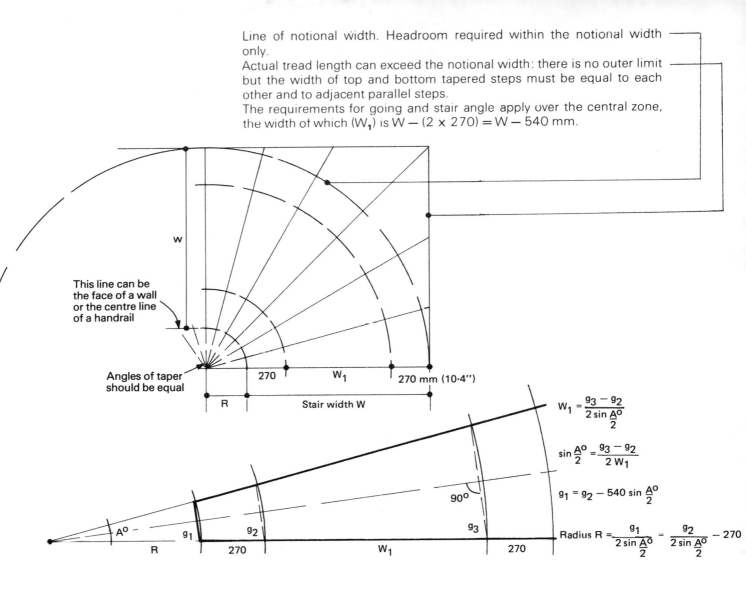

This line can be the face of a wall or the centre line of a handrail

Angles of taper should be equal

270   W_1 270 mm (10.4″)

R   Stair width W

$$W_1 = \frac{g_3 - g_2}{2 \sin \frac{A^o}{2}}$$

$$\sin \frac{A^o}{2} = \frac{g_3 - g_2}{2 W_1}$$

$$g_1 = g_2 - 540 \sin \frac{A^o}{2}$$

$$\text{Radius } R = \frac{g_1}{2 \sin \frac{A^o}{2}} = \frac{g_2}{2 \sin \frac{A^o}{2}} - 270$$

To find the maximum g_3 permitted:

$2r + g_3 =$ not more than 700

$\therefore \quad g_3 =$ not more than $700 - (2 \times 180)$

$g_3 = 340$ mm.

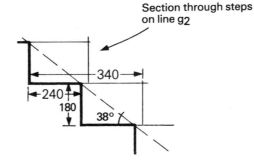

Section through steps on line g2

340

240

180   38°

The table below shows the maximum angle A° for various stair widths for the steepest common stair (38° pitch and 230 mm g_1).

W mm	W_1	g_2	g_3	$\sin \frac{A^o}{2}$	$\frac{A^o}{2}$	A°	g_1	R
800	260 mm	240 mm	340	0.2500	14°–26′	28°–52′	95 mm	190
850	310	240	340	0.2096	12°– 6′	24°–12′	117	279
900	360	240	340	0.1805	10°–24′	20°–48′	132	367
950	410	240	340	0.1585	9°– 8′	18°–16′	144	454
1000	460	240	340	0.1413	8°– 7′	16°–14′	154	545
1050	510	240	340	0.1274	7°–20′	14°–40′	161	632
1100	560	240	340	0.1160	6°–40′	13°–20′	167	720

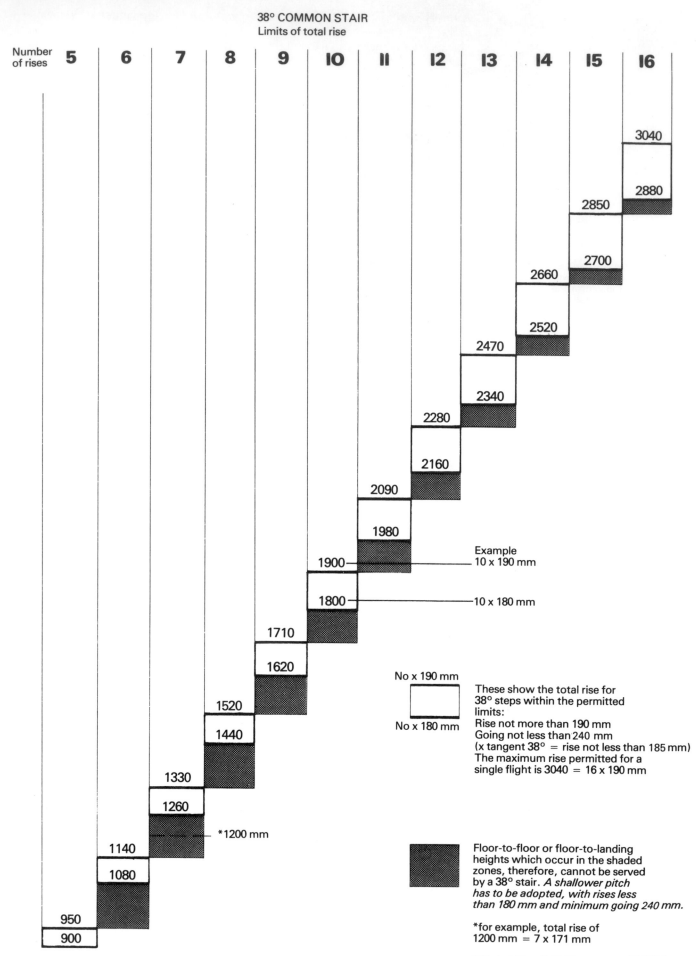

38° COMMON STAIR
Limits of total rise

| Number of rises | 5 | 6 | 7 | 8 | 9 | 10 | 11 | 12 | 13 | 14 | 15 | 16 |

Example
10 x 190 mm

10 x 180 mm

No x 190 mm

No x 180 mm

These show the total rise for 38° steps within the permitted limits:
Rise not more than 190 mm
Going not less than 240 mm
(x tangent 38° = rise not less than 185 mm)
The maximum rise permitted for a single flight is 3040 = 16 x 190 mm

Floor-to-floor or floor-to-landing heights which occur in the shaded zones, therefore, cannot be served by a 38° stair. *A shallower pitch has to be adopted, with rises less than 180 mm and minimum going 240 mm.*

*for example, total rise of 1200 mm = 7 x 171 mm

171 ÷ 240 = 0.7125 = tangent 35° 28'

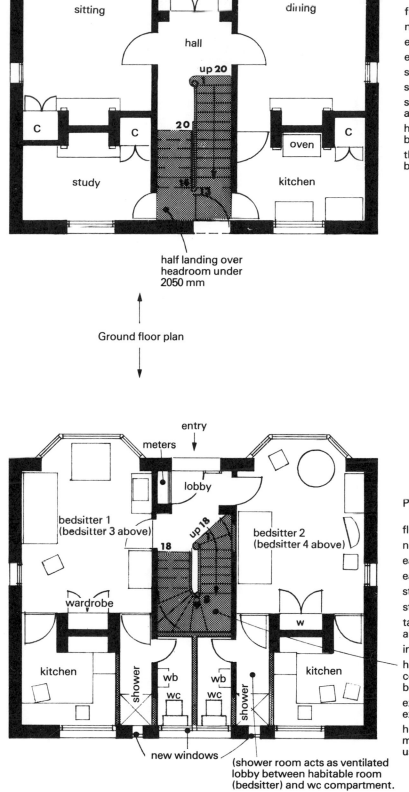

case 3: common stair

EXISTING large 2 storey (detached) one-family house.

floor to floor height	3400 mm
number of rises	20
each rise	170 mm
each going	250 mm
stair angle	34°
stair width	950 mm

spacious stair occupies a large floor area

house to be converted to 4 bedsitters (2 per floor)

the stair up to bedsitters 3 and 4 will be a 'common' stair

entry

porch

sitting

dining

hall

up 20

C

C

oven

C

20

study

kitchen

half landing over headroom under 2050 mm

Ground floor plan

entry

meters

lobby

bedsitter 1
(bedsitter 3 above)

up 18

bedsitter 2
(bedsitter 4 above)

18

wardrobe

w

kitchen

shower

wb

wb

shower

kitchen

wc

wc

new windows

(shower room acts as ventilated lobby between habitable room (bedsitter) and wc compartment.

PROPOSED converted into 4 bedsitters

floor to floor height	3400 mm
number of rises (total)	18
each rise	189 mm
each going (parallel steps)	242 mm
stair angle	38°
stair width	900 mm
tapered steps:	
angle of taper	20° 48'
internal radius	367 mm

half-landing is required as continuous flight of 18 rises would be excessive.

existing stair removed and first floor extended over part area.

high-quality balustrades and mouldings from old stair could be used on new stair.

Typical floor plan

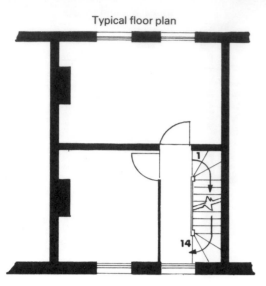

EXISTING
3 storey terrace house
floor to floor height 2880 mm
stair:
14 rises x 205 mm
approx 45° pitch
3 winders at top and bottom of each flight
800 mm wide

PROPOSED
converted to 3 flats with new spiral-stair in framed extension.
existing stairs taken out and floor extended over.
shower room acts as ventilated lobby between kitchen and wc.

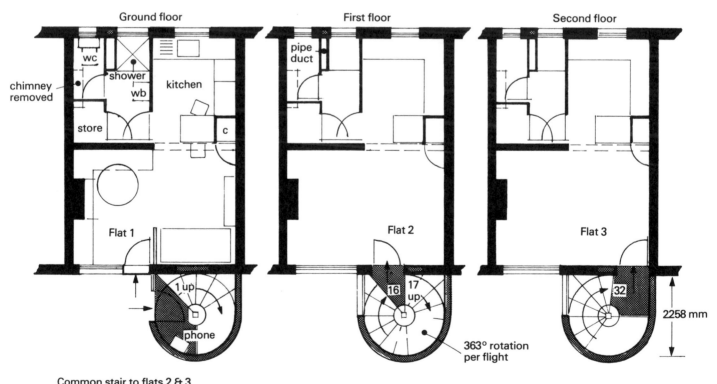

Common stair to flats 2 & 3
(refer to 'tapered steps' (b) page 74   16 rises x 180 mm = 2880 mm = floor to floor height
                                          16 rises maximum permitted in single flight (= 15 goings)

take notional stair width of 900 mm from table on p. 76
the angle of taper for 850 mm width is 24° 12'. 24° 12 x 15 goings = 363° per flight
internal radius = 279 mm. Therefore overall diameter of stair = (850 x 2) + (279 x 2) = 2258 mm

First floor plan

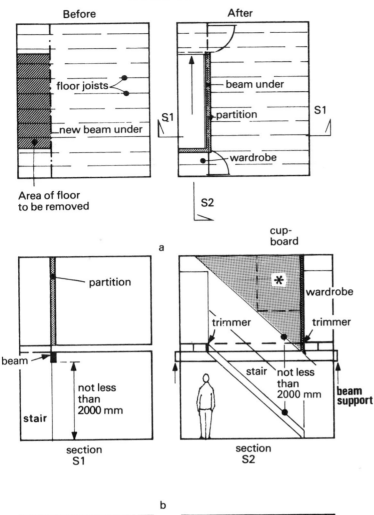

Before

After

floor joists

new beam under

Area of floor
to be removed

beam under

partition

wardrobe

S1

S1

S2

1. Stair at right angle to joists

The considerable length of a straight flight stair with top and bottom landings (see the tables for 42° private stair or 38° common stair) will, in most cases, result in the plan shown: the stair runs along the long-side and the floor joists span the shorter dimension of the room.

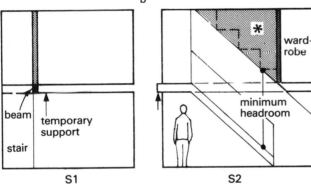

a

partition

beam

not less than 2000 mm

stair

section S1

cup-board

*

wardrobe

trimmer

trimmer

stair

not less than 2000 mm

beam support

section S2

a

The easiest method is to put a beam *under* the existing floor joists, spanning between the end walls. The stair well can then be formed by sawing through the floor (beware of cables!). The limiting factor on this is the minimum headroom of 2000 mm below the beam.

The trimmer at the top of the stair is usually made of 2 joists side by side, similarly, the trimmer to support the wardrobe partition.

b

beam

temporary support

stair

S1

*

ward-robe

minimum headroom

S2

b

Where existing headroom in the room below is not sufficient to enable a beam to be put in, then the floor must be temporarily supported whilst the stairwell is cut and the beam put into the floor depth. Use metal framing anchors to fix the joists to the beam.

*The space shaded above the minimum headroom line on section S2 can be used for storage (a cupboard is shown): the new partition must be designed to allow for the loads transmitted, and the beam under the partition.

The superimposed load in a cupboard can be assumed to be 146.5 kg/m² (30lbs/sq ft), which is the design figure for domestic floors.

First floor plan

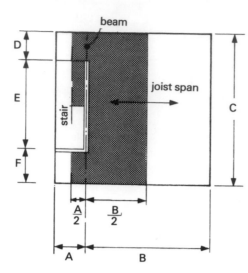

The total floor area supported by the beam =
$$(C \times \frac{B}{2}) + (D \times \frac{A}{2}) + (F \times \frac{A}{2}) + (E \times \frac{A}{2}) \text{ m}^2$$

This total area is then multiplied by (deadweight of floor + superimposed load) kg/m² to give the total floor load on the beam kg , add to this the deadweight of partitions, doors, etc., and any superimposed load on the partitions (such as shelving) to give the total uniformly distributed load on the beam.

The superimposed load on domestic floors

is taken as 146 kg/m² (30 lbs/ft²)

Weights of various materials and typical floors and partitions are given on structure (3)

First floor plan

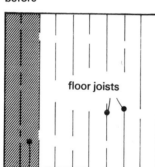

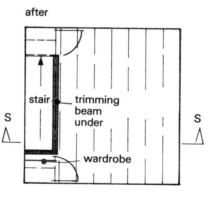

2. STAIR PARALLEL TO FLOOR JOISTS

Cut back the floorboards and ceiling over the proposed stair area, and remove the exposed joists. Two of these can be used side by side, as the floor trimming beam.
However, if a partition is to be built, it may be necessary to put in a deeper-section beam in place of the double joist.

The trimming beam supports the following loads: —

i the partition alongside the stair
ii ½ of the top landing (the other ½ supported on the side wall).
iii ½ of the wardrobe floor and ½ of the partition over the stair (the other half supported on the side wall).
iv ¼ of the stair, assuming that each side stringer carries ½ the load.
The top support of each stringer carries ½ the load of each stringer.

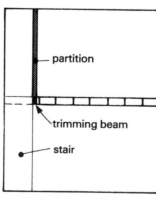

section S

		Thickness mm	Structure (3) Weight kg/m²
softwood boarding		19	9.1
		22	11.0
		25	1.0
plywood	Douglas fir	12.5	6.7
	British made	12.5	7.8
	Finnish birch	12.5	8.7
	European beech	12.5	9.3
	blockboard	25	10.2
wood chipboard		12.5	9.6
		19	14.6
		22	16.1
low density extruded		50	9.0
hardboard		3.2	3.0 to 3.3
(weight varies according		4.8	4.3 to 4.8
to brand)		6.4	5.7 to 6.6
medium board		6	4.4 to 4.6
(weight varies according		9	6.3 to 6.8
to brand)		12	7.3 to 8.9
fibre insulation board		9.5	2.5 to 2.7
(weight varies according		12.7	3.2 to 3.7
to brand)		19	4.4 to 5.4
		25	6.4 to 7.6
gypsum plasterboard		9.5	8.5
		12.5	11.2
		19	17.1
corkboard		25	4.9
woodwool slab		25	14.6
asbestos insulation board		6.4	4.6
		9.5	6.7
		12.7	9.2
mineral-wool quilt		25	3.4
		50	6.8
insulating felt		25	4.9
plaster lightweight (2 coat)		10	10
gypsum (2 coat)		13	23.4

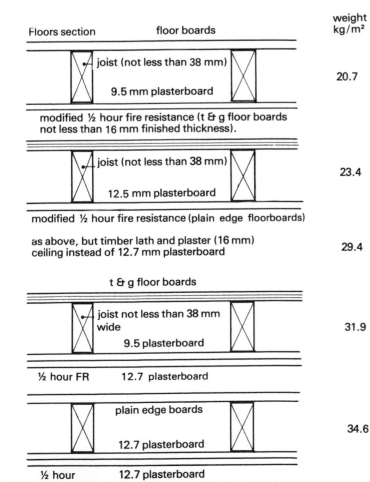

Floors section floor boards

	weight kg/m²
joist (not less than 38 mm) — 9.5 mm plasterboard	20.7

modified ½ hour fire resistance (t & g floor boards not less than 16 mm finished thickness).

| joist (not less than 38 mm) — 12.5 mm plasterboard | 23.4 |

modified ½ hour fire resistance (plain edge floorboards)

as above, but timber lath and plaster (16 mm) ceiling instead of 12.7 mm plasterboard — 29.4

t & g floor boards

| joist not less than 38 mm wide — 9.5 plasterboard | 31.9 |

½ hour FR   12.7 plasterboard

| plain edge boards — 12.7 plasterboard | 34.6 |

½ hour   12.7 plasterboard

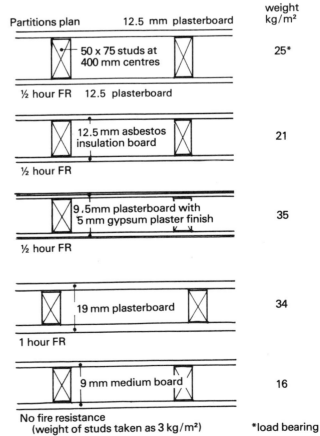

Partitions plan   12.5 mm plasterboard

	weight kg/m²
50 x 75 studs at 400 mm centres	25*

½ hour FR   12.5 plasterboard

| 12.5 mm asbestos insulation board | 21 |

½ hour FR

| 9.5mm plasterboard with 5 mm gypsum plaster finish | 35 |

½ hour FR

| 19 mm plasterboard | 34 |

1 hour FR

| 9 mm medium board | 16 |

No fire resistance
(weight of studs taken as 3 kg/m²)   *load bearing

Planning kitchens, bathrooms and toilets

The requirements shown under the heading 'Building Regulations' apply to the proposed construction of a house, or an extension to an existing house, or to the construction of a kitchen or bathroom etc, inside an existing house.

They do not apply to an existing kitchen or bathroom etc, which will be unaffected by any building work or alterations to an existing house.

None of the dimensions shown on the layouts are mandatory in home improvements or extensions, although improvements to council houses are usually carried out in order to up-grade them to Parker Morris standards.

The layouts shown are intended for guidance and obviously will not suit every situation.

In some cases, careful design can enable the dimensions shown to be reduced, eg by using sliding doors, of concealing a WC cistern in an adjoining cupboard.

The floor area and perimeter wall length of each layout is shown, and an indication of which plans have economical plumbing layouts. Costs will be minimised if floor area, wall length and plumbing are at a minimum.

The planning dimensions are taken from the following references:

- Design Bulletin No 6 (Metric 1968) 'Space in the Home' MOHLG (now DoE) recommendations of the Parker Morris Committee Report.
- Design Bulletin No 24 Part 1, 1972 'Bathrooms & WC's (DoE)
- Design Bulletin No 24 Part 2, 'Kitchens' (DoE)

KITCHEN requirements

'Homes for today and tomorrow' 1961 by the Parker Morris Committee recommended minimum space standards, illustrated in DB6 'Space in the Home':
Kitchen layout should include uninterrupted sequence of worktop/cooker/worktop/sink/worktop. Space for refrigerator and washing machine required; this can be under worktops. Suitable layouts and clearances are shown below.

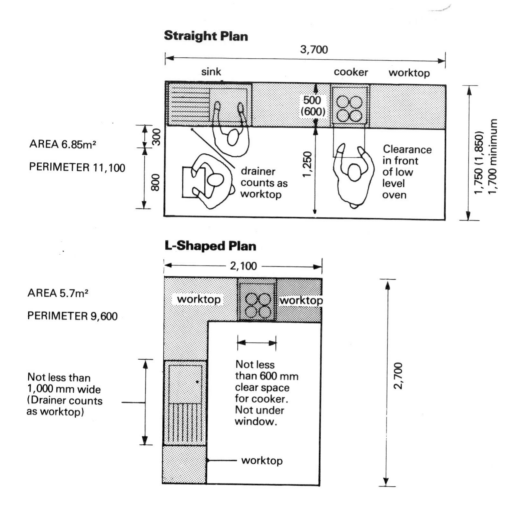

Straight Plan

3,700

sink   cooker worktop

500 (600)

1,250

AREA 6.85m²

PERIMETER 11,100

300

800

drainer counts as worktop

Clearance in front of low level oven

1,750 (1,850) 1,700 minimum

L-Shaped Plan

2,100

AREA 5.7m²

PERIMETER 9,600

worktop   worktop

Not less than 600 mm clear space for cooker. Not under window.

Not less than 1,000 mm wide (Drainer counts as worktop)

2,700

worktop

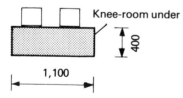

Knee-room under

400

1,100

The Kitchen in a dwelling for 2 or more persons must contain a counter top or space for a table where at least 2 people can eat casual meals.
The kitchen must contain at least 1.7 m³ enclosed storage space in a 1 or 2 person dwelling, or 2.3 m³ in a dwelling for 3 or more persons.
Included in this storage requirement is a ventilated 'cool' cupboard and a broom cupboard, which can be elsewhere.
Linen Storage 0.4 m³ cupboard space is required in a dwelling for 1, 2 or 3 persons.
0.6 m³ required in dwelling for more persons.

THE BUILDING REGULATIONS, 1976
(A summary of the internal requirements)

Regulation A4 (1)
Definition

The term 'habitable room' does not apply to a kitchen or scullery, where food is stored, prepared and cooked. However, if there is provision for eating the food in the kitchen (as recommended in DoE Design Bulletin 24 Part 2) the kitchen might be considered by some authorities to be a 'habitable room'. In this case, 2300 mm (7 ft 6½ in) ceiling height is required although a bay window or beam can be less than this but not lower than 2000 mm (6 ft 7 in).

Regulation K8 (1)
Ceiling Height

Regulation K4 (1)
Ventilation

K4 (1) In this regulation 'habitable room' definitely includes a kitchen. The total area of all openable windows, hinged panels, louvres or vents direct to external air shall be more than 1/20th the floor area of the room. Some part of this vent area must be not less than 1750 mm (5 ft 9 in) above the floor.

Regulation K4 (3)

Regulation K4 (4)

The total area of a door which opens directly to external air may be counted as part of the total area stated in K4 (3) providing that a the door contains a ventilator at least 10000 mm² (16 sq in) in area which can be opened while the door is shut or b the room contains one or more separate vents of at least 10000 mm² (16 sq in) total area.

(These areas do not apply if there is adequate mechanical ventilation). If kitchen ventilates into a court enclosed on every side, refer to Regulation K5.

Regulation K6
Ventilation of larders

Any larder for the storage of perishable food shall be ventilated to the external air either by adequate mechanical means or by
a one or more windows, or
b two or more ventilators, capable of being closed, one at high level, one at low level.

Any vent must have a durable fly-proof screen, and an opening area of at least 4500 mm² (7 sq in). A duct to external air is permitted from a vent. The duct must have smooth internal lining and a cross sectional area of at least 16000 mm² (25 sq in).

Any window must have a durable fly-proof screen, and an opening area of at least 85000 mm² (136 sq in).

'PROVISION OF SPACE FOR DOMESTIC KITCHEN EQUIPMENT'
(BS 3705 : 1972)
recommended width (front to back) : worktop, sink unit 600 mm
recommended height   „   „   900 mm
recommended length of sink units 1200, 1500, 1800 mm
BS range of storage units:
base units 600 wide × 900 high × 400, 500, 600, 800, 1000, 1200 mm long
tall units 600 wide × 1950, 2250 high × 500, 600 mm long
wall units 300 wide × 600, 900 high × 400, 500, 600, 800, 1000 1200 mm long
minimum length of space required for cooker or fridge or washing machine or spin dryer or dishwasher is 600 mm.

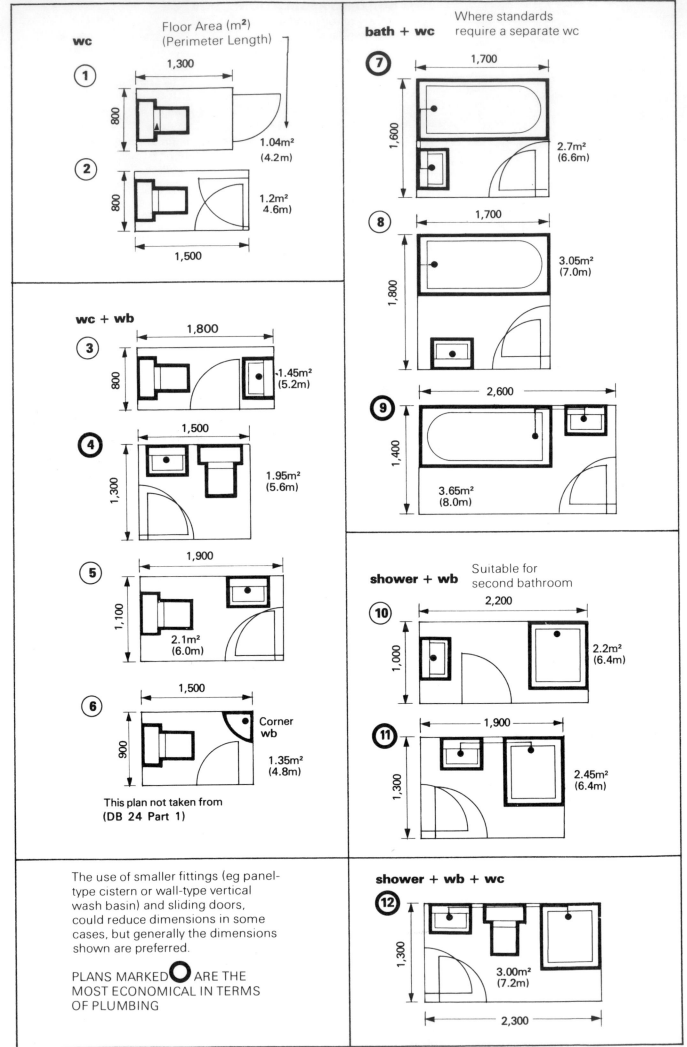

wc

Floor Area (m²)
(Perimeter Length)

① 1,300 / 800 — 1.04m² (4.2m)

② 800 / 1,500 — 1.2m² 4.6m

wc + wb

③ 1,800 / 800 — 1.45m² (5.2m)

④ 1,500 / 1,300 — 1.95m² (5.6m)

⑤ 1,900 / 1,100 — 2.1m² (6.0m)

⑥ 1,500 / 900 — Corner wb — 1.35m² (4.8m)

This plan not taken from
(DB 24 Part 1)

bath + wc Where standards require a separate wc

⑦ 1,700 / 1,600 — 2.7m² (6.6m)

⑧ 1,700 / 1,800 — 3.05m² (7.0m)

⑨ 2,600 / 1,400 — 3.65m² (8.0m)

shower + wb Suitable for second bathroom

⑩ 2,200 / 1,000 — 2.2m² (6.4m)

⑪ 1,900 / 1,300 — 2.45m² (6.4m)

shower + wb + wc

⑫ 1,300 / 3.00m² (7.2m) / 2,300

The use of smaller fittings (eg panel-type cistern or wall-type vertical wash basin) and sliding doors, could reduce dimensions in some cases, but generally the dimensions shown are preferred.

PLANS MARKED ⬤ ARE THE MOST ECONOMICAL IN TERMS OF PLUMBING

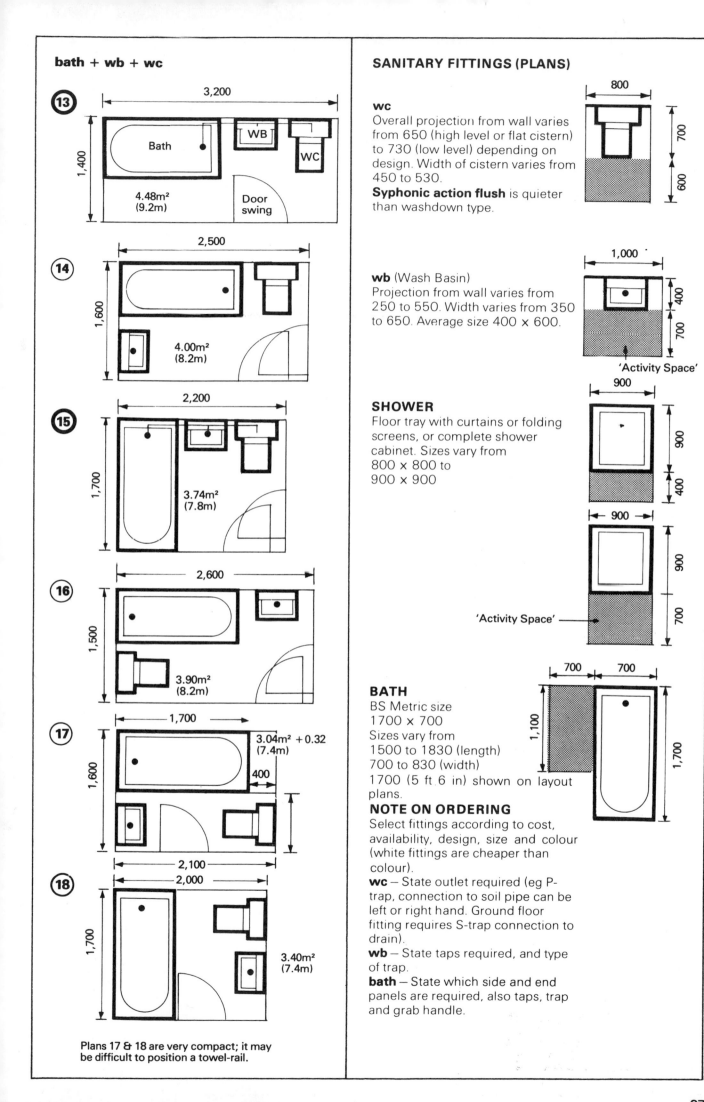

bath + wb + wc

(13)
3,200
1,400
Bath
WB
WC
4.48m² (9.2m)
Door swing

(14)
2,500
1,600
4.00m² (8.2m)

(15)
2,200
1,700
3.74m² (7.8m)

(16)
2,600
1,500
3.90m² (8.2m)

(17)
1,700
1,600
3.04m² + 0.32 (7.4m)
400

(18)
2,100
2,000
1,700
3.40m² (7.4m)

Plans 17 & 18 are very compact; it may be difficult to position a towel-rail.

SANITARY FITTINGS (PLANS)

wc

Overall projection from wall varies from 650 (high level or flat cistern) to 730 (low level) depending on design. Width of cistern varies from 450 to 530.
Syphonic action flush is quieter than washdown type.

800
700
600

wb (Wash Basin)

Projection from wall varies from 250 to 550. Width varies from 350 to 650. Average size 400 x 600.

1,000
400
700
'Activity Space'

SHOWER

Floor tray with curtains or folding screens, or complete shower cabinet. Sizes vary from 800 x 800 to 900 x 900

900
900
400

900
900
700
'Activity Space'

BATH

BS Metric size 1700 x 700
Sizes vary from
1500 to 1830 (length)
700 to 830 (width)
1700 (5 ft.6 in) shown on layout plans.

700   700
1,100
1,700

NOTE ON ORDERING

Select fittings according to cost, availability, design, size and colour (white fittings are cheaper than colour).
wc – State outlet required (eg P-trap, connection to soil pipe can be left or right hand. Ground floor fitting requires S-trap connection to drain).
wb – State taps required, and type of trap.
bath – State which side and end panels are required, also taps, trap and grab handle.

BATHROOM & WC requirements

THE BUILDING REGULATIONS 1976
Part N and Part P 'Sanitary Conveniences' (Summary)

P1 wc to be smooth, non absorbent surface, discharging through an effective trap to a soil pipe or drain. Flushing to provide effective cleaning.

No part of wc to connect with any pipe except soil pipe, flush pipe, trap vent pipe or drain.

N4 (2) Internal diameter of wc outlet and soil pipe should be not less than 75 mm.

N4 (3) Internal diameter of wash basin waste pipe should be not less than 32 mm.

P3 (1) 'SANITARY ACCOMMODATION' means a room containing a wc or urinal fittings, whether or not it contains other sanitary fittings.

P3 (2) No sanitary accommodation shall open directly into

a A habitable room; ✱ except a bedroom or dressing-room ★

b A kitchen or scullery

c Workroom — manufacture, trade or business.

P3 (3) Requires second door into toilet in case of P3 (2) (a), from a room not used for sleeping or dressing, unless there is a second wc in the dwelling not entered through any such room. An outside toilet serving a private dwelling house will satisfy this.

P3 (4) VENTILATION OF THE SANITARY ACCOMMODATION

a Window, skylight or other vent, opening directly to external air, minimum opening area 1/20th of floor area. ★

b Mechanical ventilation direct to external air, minimum 3 air changes per hour.

LOCAL AUTHORITY HOUSING (MOHLG CIRCULAR 1/68)

a In 1 person, 2 person and 3 person dwellings, 1 wc required; can be in bathroom.

b In 4 person, 2- or 3-storey houses and 2-storey maisonettes, 1 wc required in separate compartment.

In 4 person and 5 person flats and bungalows, 1 wc required in separate compartment.

c In 2- or 3-storey houses and 2-storey maisonettes at or above minimum floor area for 5 persons (86.5 m², 98.5 m², 85.5 m² respectively including general storage) 2 wc's required, one of which may be in bathroom. Ditto for flat or bungalow at or above minimum floor area for 6 persons (90.0 and 88.5 m²).

d wb required in wc compartment unless the bathroom is adjoining.

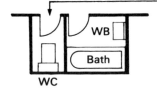

WB

Bath

WC

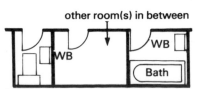

other room(s) in between

WB

WB

Bath

WC

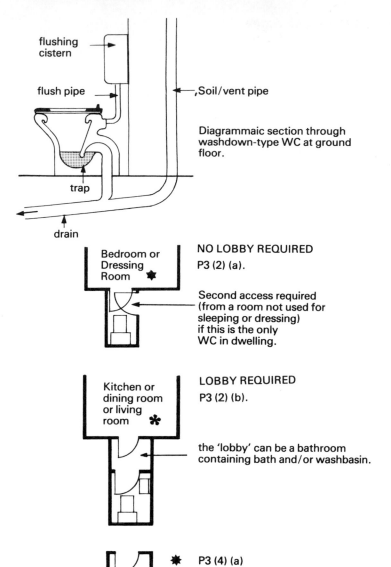

flushing cistern

flush pipe

,Soil/vent pipe

Diagrammaic section through washdown-type WC at ground floor.

trap

drain

Bedroom or Dressing Room ✸

NO LOBBY REQUIRED
P3 (2) (a).

Second access required (from a room not used for sleeping or dressing) if this is the only WC in dwelling.

Kitchen or dining room or living room ✿

LOBBY REQUIRED
P3 (2) (b).

the 'lobby' can be a bathroom containing bath and/or washbasin.

✸ P3 (4) (a)

Opening area measured in elevation to be not less than A + 20.

PRIVATE HOUSING

(NHBRC Handbook 1970) (National House-Builders Registration Council) (now NHBC).

Each dwelling shall have at least 1 wc, 1 bath or shower, 1wb and 1 sink.

Any dwelling with an internal staircase and floor area more than 80 m², or any flat or bungalow more than 75 m², must have 1 wc in separate compartment, as a minimum.

wb required in wc compartment unless the bathroom is adjoining.

9

External appearance

The external appearance of a house undergoing improvement is not always considered. The advice that follows is based on the simple view that alterations to an old house should improve it or, at least, not spoil it. Alas, this is not usually the case. Here is a typical example:

fig. 1

BEFORE

Chimney

Clay pantiles

Brickwork verge

Vertical proportion windows, set back in wall

Wall details, e.g. brick arches, quoins

fig. 2

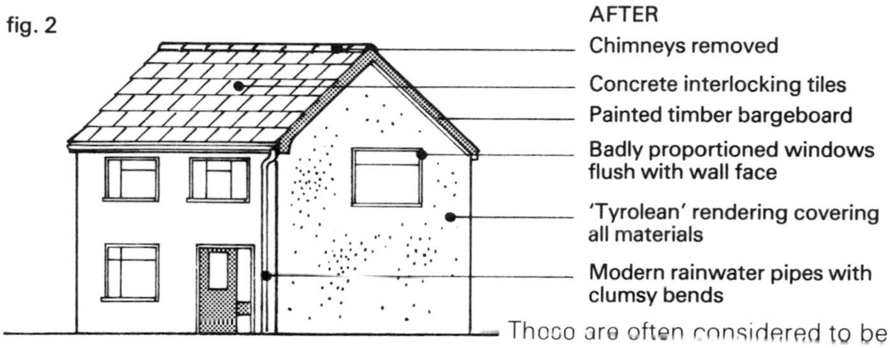

AFTER

Chimneys removed

Concrete interlocking tiles

Painted timber bargeboard

Badly proportioned windows flush with wall face

'Tyrolean' rendering covering all materials

Modern rainwater pipes with clumsy bends

These are often considered to be improvements by most people involved in this work. They usually give the following reasons:

1 The old materials were dilapidated and let in the rain.
2 The new materials are cheap, readily available and easy to fix.
3 The bigger windows let in more light and air.
4 The modernised house looks like a new house.

But they ignore some rather more important facts:

1 Many people like old houses because they do not look like new houses (and many new houses are badly designed anyway).
2 Larger windows let out more heat than small ones, and have less privacy inside.
3 Rendering over wall-surfaces may make existing dampness worse.
4 Well-proportioned windows and sympathetic materials cost no more than any others.

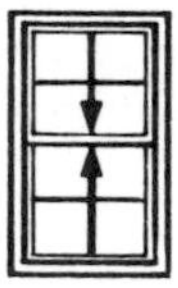

WINDOWS are probably the most important visual elements on an elevation; the majority of modernised houses and new houses are spoilt by the use of certain badly designed standard windows (illustrated later). The fault is basically that they are manufactured and installed with no reference to the appearance of the building. Traditionally, some thought was given by builders to the size and position of windows (for instance, those facing south could be larger than those facing the north wind). Windows and door-frames were usually set back from the face of the wall to protect them against the weather. These commonsense points are generally ignored nowadays, and this inevitably results in more rapid decay and failure. The shape of a window was usually determined by the limiting span of a timber lintel. No such restriction limited the height however, and so a vertical shape was most common (fig 3).
Wider openings were made possible by the use of loadbearing mullions, which also gave a vertical emphasis (fig 4).
Opening frames were side hung casements, and the structural cantilever again limited the width (fig 5).
The vertical sliding sash introduced in the 18th Century, also had vertical proportions (fig 6).

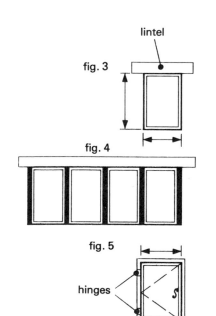

lintel

fig. 3

fig. 4

fig. 5

hinges

fig. 6

The attractive appearance of Georgian houses is due to the regularity and proportion of their windows, and the contrast between the verticals (windows, door, chimneys) and the horizontals (brick courses and mouldings). Victorian terrace houses have similar attractive contrasts:

fig. 7

fig. 8

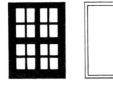

Improvements can be made by replacing the old window frames and doors (which were often ugly) with modern, simple windows and doors in the existing structural opening (fig 8).

Modern window openings are no longer limited in width, due to the use of steel or reinforced concrete lintels, and the large sizes of glass available. In some modern houses, the wide window is perfectly acceptable (especially if there is a panoramic view), but in many houses and particularly in 'improved' houses it is out of place.

The massive heat loss through a large window is not sufficiently considered until the first winter after occupation, and then expensive remedial action has to be taken (much to the delight of the double glazing trade). The lack of privacy is another factor rarely considered (fig 9):

fig. 9
PLAN

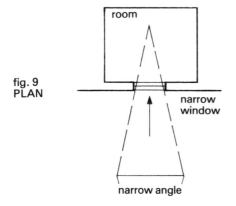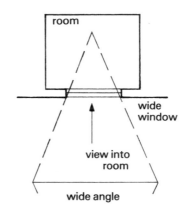

There are also the practical problems involved in widening an existing opening, which can prove costly.

Therefore, if more daylight and/or ventilation is required in any existing room, consider the following alternatives instead of widening the window:

a Replace a small paned, thick frame with a light modern one (fig 10). This may give up to 25 per cent extra daylight.

b Lower the sill height and put in a deeper window.

c Put an additional window in a new opening matching the existing.

Modern window frames (in timber, aluminium, steel or plastics) vary enormously in the standard of design, the ease of operation, the cost of maintaining them, and the capital cost. Painted frames of steel or timber are more expensive to maintain than anodised aluminium; or plastics-coated steel or timber; or timber finished with a water-repellent stain. The proportions are very important, and it is advisable not to use the following patterns (fig 11).

fig. 10

fig. 11

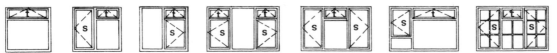

t — top hung
s — side hung

These are badly proportioned because they are either of horizontal emphasis, or divided into two or more unrelated areas which may have top hung and side hung opening frames in the same window, giving a chaotic effect when opened. The last one, by adding small glazing-bars between the main members (which still can be seen because of their greater thickness) results in:

1 A reduction in the amount of daylight getting through.
2 An interference with the view out.
3 An increase in the cost of the window.
4 An increase in the cost of the glazing.
5 An increase in the cost of painting each window frame.

The following patterns, from the same standard ranges of window frames, are better, because they will not have a disruptive effect on a house elevation, even when opened (fig 12).

fig. 12

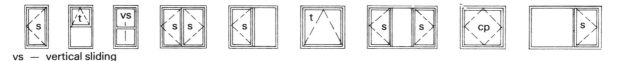

vs — vertical sliding
cp — centre pivot

cross section
fig. 13

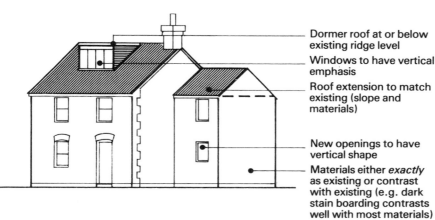

limited ventilation

However, side hung casement windows have the disadvantage that they let in driving rain (and housebreakers) when open. This is not the case with the top hung 'fanlights' featured in fig 11. However, these do not let in much air either (fig 13).

The same amount of ventilation can be provided by a night-vent or louvre set into a casement or fixed pane.

SUMMARY OF RECOMMENDATIONS

1 Roof

a Re-use the existing materials if possible, after fixing a good quality tiling felt over the rafters, which acts as a waterproof barrier (so it does not matter if the old claytiles or slates etc are not close-fitting). Incorporate new tiling battens that have been preservative treated.

b Avoid artificial-coloured materials.

c Choose rainwater goods carefully, as some systems have badly designed angles and joints.

d Do not add bargeboards at gable ends if there were none before.

2 Walls

a Repair the existing materials if possible. (Refer to the chapter 'Dealing with dampness')

b Avoid the use of 'blanket' materials such as cement rendering or spray coatings, especially those which collect dirt quickly and look dull and shabby.

3 Windows

a Repair the existing frames if possible.

b Do not widen the existing openings.

c Select new frames which have vertical proportions and are not divided into different opening lights.

d Set the frames back from the face of the wall.

e Use durable materials: steel frames to be rust proofed, timber frames to be preservative-treated and preferably finished with water repellent stain rather than paint and the concealed faces to be protected by a dpc.

f Window sills should be of stone, slate, brick or tile rather than painted timber.

4 Extensions

Dormer roof at or below existing ridge level

Windows to have vertical emphasis

Roof extension to match existing (slope and materials)

New openings to have vertical shape

Materials either *exactly* as existing or contrast with existing (e.g. dark stain boarding contrasts well with most materials)

Extensions and the Building Regulations

10

Extensions to an existing building are 'new work' and so Parts A to P of the Building Regulations apply.

Part K — 'Open space, ventilation and height of habitable rooms' — is of prime importance because it can limit the size of the extension (irrespective of the constructional materials used).

Part K is summarised as follows:

EXTENSION TO EXISTING BUILDING 'NO CHANGE OF USE'

Regulation K3 permits an extension which provides a 'kitchen, scullery, washroom, watercloset or bathroom' to be built — at the rear of a private dwelling house erected 'under former control' (ie before 1st February 1966) — if there remains an area of not less than 9 m² adjacent to the extension and exclusively belonging to it; for example:

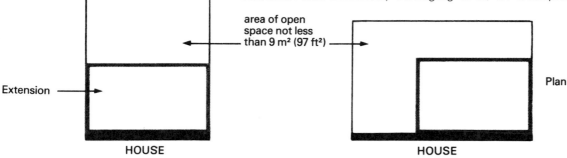

If the extension provides accommodation not listed above, then it is limited in size by its proximity to an existing habitable room window: the requirement is that 'no building shall be so altered or extended as to cause the zone of open space outside the window or windows of any habitable room in the building to contravene the provisions of Regulation K1, or (if that zone already contravenes these provisions) to cause the zone to contravene the provisions to any greater extent'. This 'let-out' clause applies only where there is 'no change of use'.

Regulation K1 applies fully to the extension and to the 'existing' when there is a 'change of use' from PG I to PG III.

Regulation K1

'Zones of open space' — the zone is a vertical shaft of space open to the sky adjacent to a window of a habitable room.

(NB glass blocks are not classed as a window).

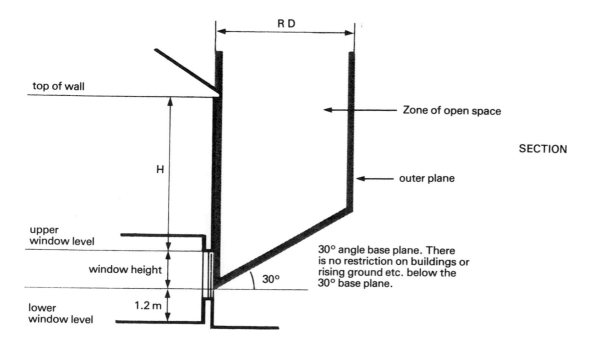

Definitions:
'top of wall' — underside of flat roof or pitched roof eaves or top of parapet.
'upper window level' — the highest level of glass in the window.
'lower window level' — the lowest level of glass in the window, 1.2 m above the floor level, whichever is higher.
Required Distance (RD) — It must be at least 3.6 m (11 ft 10 in) OR $H \div 2$, whichever is the greater, up to a maximum of 15 m (49 ft 3 in). The 3.6 m limit will apply unless H exceeds 7.2 m which would probably occur only in buildings of more than 3-storeys.

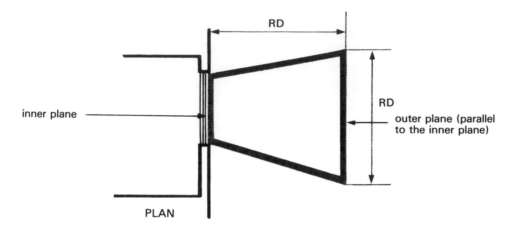

PLAN

The 'inner plane' coincides with the external face of a wall whether or not there is a projecting bay window.
The width of the 'inner plane'
= the floor area of the room $\div$ (10 x the window height).
This may be less than or more than the actual width of the window:

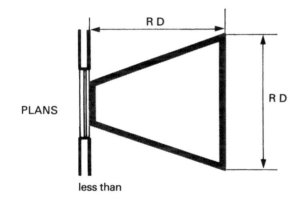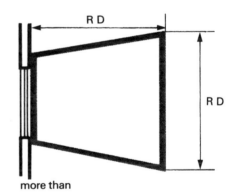

PLANS   less than   more than

Regulation K1 (4)
Where a habitable room contains two or more windows, the 'zone of open space' may be provided outside any of them so that the total of (inner plane width x window height) = not less than (the floor area $\div$ 10).

PLAN

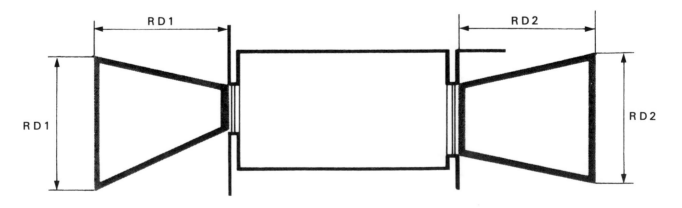

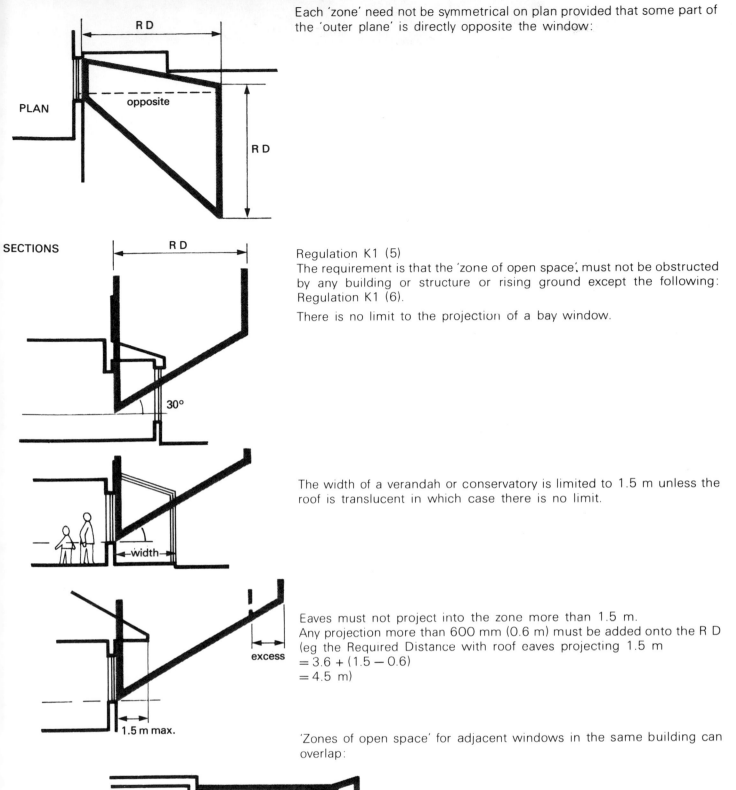

Each 'zone' need not be symmetrical on plan provided that some part of the 'outer plane' is directly opposite the window:

PLAN

opposite

SECTIONS

Regulation K1 (5)
The requirement is that the 'zone of open space' must not be obstructed by any building or structure or rising ground except the following: Regulation K1 (6).

There is no limit to the projection of a bay window.

The width of a verandah or conservatory is limited to 1.5 m unless the roof is translucent in which case there is no limit.

Eaves must not project into the zone more than 1.5 m.
Any projection more than 600 mm (0.6 m) must be added onto the R D
(eg the Required Distance with roof eaves projecting 1.5 m
$= 3.6 + (1.5 - 0.6)$
$= 4.5$ m)

'Zones of open space' for adjacent windows in the same building can overlap:

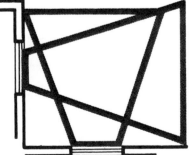

PLAN

'Zones of open space' for adjacent buildings must not overlap.
The 'zone of open space' must be situated wholly over land exclusively belonging:
Regulation K1 (5)
to the building*
or
over an adjoining street, canal or river, but only as far as its centre line*

*See over

or

Regulation K2

over shared land on housing estates

or

over a combination of these.

*These requirements have the effect of prohibiting a 'habitable room' window which faces a shared boundary less than 3.6 m away OR which faces a street, canal or river whose centre line is less than 3.6 m from the external wall face OR which faces a 'habitable room' window in a building less than 7.2 m away across shared land, unless the 'zones of open space' are staggered on plan:

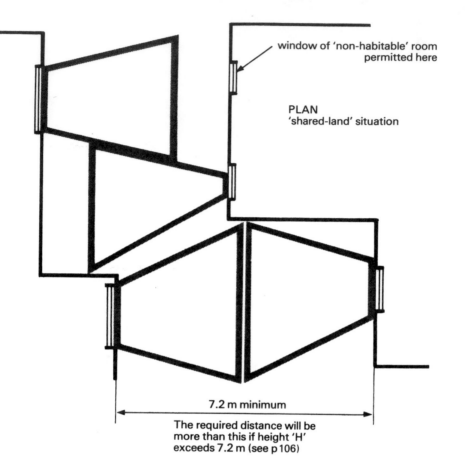

window of 'non-habitable' room
permitted here

PLAN
'shared-land' situation

7.2 m minimum

The required distance will be more than this if height 'H' exceeds 7.2 m (see p 106)

Regulation K4

Means of ventilation

— Applies to 'new work' where there is 'no change of use', subject to the requirement about not adversely affecting the 'existing'.

— Applies to 'new work' and to 'existing' where there is 'change of use' from Purpose Group I to Purpose Group III.

Regulation K4 (3)

The requirements are that a 'habitable room' unless it has adequate mechanical ventilation, must have one or more 'ventilation openings', whose total area = not less than the room's floor area ÷ 20.

Part of the ventilation opening must be at least 1.75 m (5 ft 9 in) above the floor.

'Habitable room' — bedroom, living room, dining room, study, kitchen or scullery.

(NB These last two are not classed as 'habitable rooms' in Regulation K1, or K3 or K8)

'Ventilation opening' — any openable part of a window or any hinged panel, adjustable louvre or air-bricks, except any opening associated with a mechanically operated system.

Regulation K4 (4)

The total area of a door which opens directly to external air may be counted as part of the total area required in K4 (3), if:

a the door contains a ventilator at least 10,000 mm² (16 in²) in area which can be opened while the door is shut

or

b the room contains one or more separate vents of at least 10,000 mm² (16 in²) total area.

Regulation K6

Ventilation of larders

There is no requirement that a larder should be provided, and the development of refrigerators and deep-freezers has made larders unnecessary. However, if it is decided to provide a larder for the storage of perishable food or, more likely, to keep an existing larder when a Purpose Group I house is converted to Purpose Group III use, then K6 applies: unless there is adequate mechanical ventilation, a larder for perishable food must be ventilated to the external air by
a one or more windows with durable flyproof screen(s)
The total window area must be at least 85,000 mm² (136 in²)
or
b two or more ventilators, capable of being closed, one at high level, one at low level. Each vent must have a durable flyproof screen and an unobstructed opening of not less than 4500 mm² (7 in²).
A duct to external air is permitted from a ventilator, provided the duct has smooth internal lining and a cross sectional area of at least 16,000 mm² (25 in²).

Regulation K5

Ventilation openings onto courts

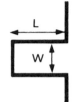

The ventilation openings specified in K4 can be positioned in any side of a court (ie an open space surrounded by buildings) if the width of the court is 15 m or more, OR (in the case of a court open on one side) if the length is less than twice the width.
Where the court does not satisfy these limits, then apply the following:

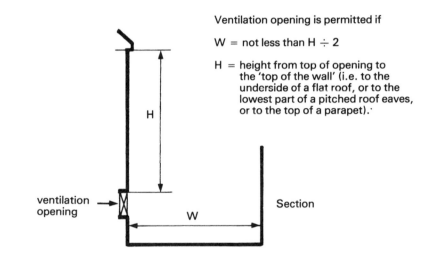

Ventilation opening is permitted if

W = not less than H ÷ 2

H = height from top of opening to the 'top of the wall' (i.e. to the underside of a flat roof, or to the lowest part of a pitched roof eaves, or to the top of a parapet).

ventilation opening

Section

In the case of a court with one short side open, and with length more than twice the width:
– a ventilation opening can be positioned in the remaining short side without restriction. It can be positioned in either of the long sides, provided that it is within a distance from the open end not exceeding 2W, or W is not less than 15 m, or W = not less than H ÷ 2 (as previously described).

Regulation K7

Ventilation of common stairways

Applies to 'new work' and 'existing' in the case of a 'change of use' from Purpose Group I to Purpose Group III.
The requirement is that any internal common stair above the ground storey 'shall have adequate means of ventilation'.

Regulation K8

Height of habitable rooms

This applies only to 'new work', whether or not a 'change of use' is involved.
It is obviously totally impracticable to apply it to the 'existing'.
The requirements are that a habitable room (not including a kitchen or scullery, unless used for eating purposes) shall have headroom not less

than 2,300 mm (7 ft 6½ in) although a bay window, beam or joist can be less but not less than 2,000 mm (6 ft 7 in).

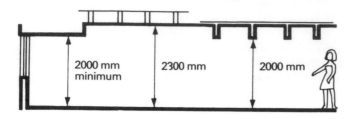

The requirements for habitable rooms in roofs are described in the chapter 'Attic conversion'.

SUMMARY OF PART K IN RELATION TO EXTENSIONS
A 'No change of use'
open space: Not less than 9 m² area required adjacent to an extended house and exclusively belonging to it, if the extension provides a kitchen, (example A1) scullery, washroom, wc or bathroom.
ventilation: kitchen or scullery Reg K4 (3)
wc or bathroom containing wc
Regulation P3 (4).
(Larder Regulation K6

} not less than 1/20th floor area

for restrictions on ventilation into court see Regulation K5.

Example A1

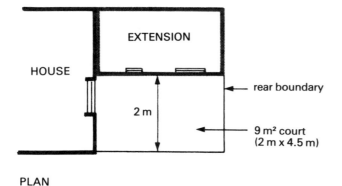

PLAN

The ventilation openings are permitted if the height above them to the top of the wall of the extension is not more than 4m (Regulation K5 (2) (b): H = not more than W x 2).

Extension providing a habitable room

Example A2

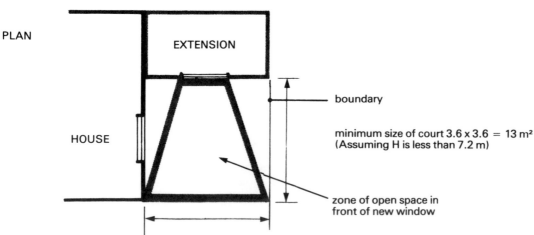

Example A3

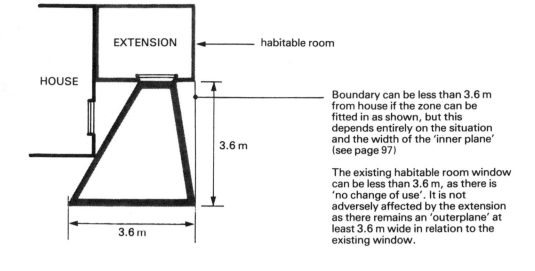

HOUSE

EXTENSION ← — habitable room

3.6 m

3.6 m

Boundary can be less than 3.6 m from house if the zone can be fitted in as shown, but this depends entirely on the situation and the width of the 'inner plane' (see page 97)

The existing habitable room window can be less than 3.6 m, as there is 'no change of use'. It is not adversely affected by the extension as there remains an 'outerplane' at least 3.6 m wide in relation to the existing window.

B 'Change of use'
'Ventilation' requirements are as in A, but they apply to existing as well as 'new work'.

Example B1

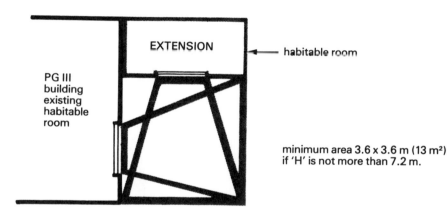

EXTENSION ← — habitable room

PG III building existing habitable room

minimum area 3.6 x 3.6 m (13 m²) if 'H' is not more than 7.2 m.

Example B2

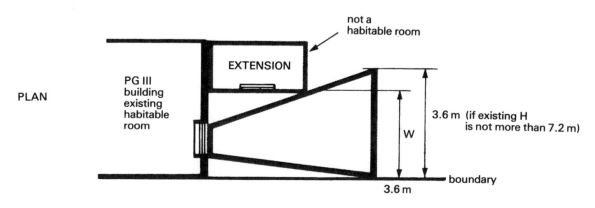

PLAN

not a habitable room

EXTENSION

PG III building existing habitable room

3.6 m (if existing H is not more than 7.2 m)

W

boundary

3.6 m

W can be less than 3.6 m if the zone can be fitted in as shown.

Position of ventilation openings in long side of extension is unrestricted if H on the extension wall is not more than W ÷ 2.

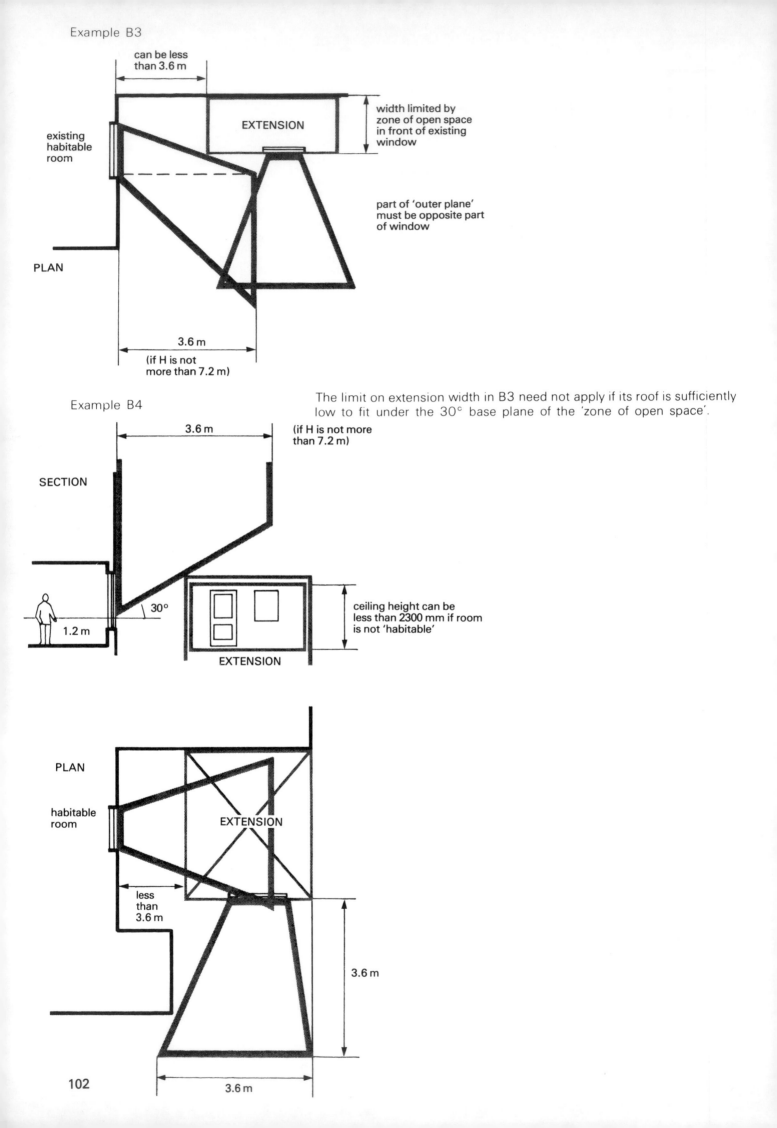

Example B3

can be less
than 3.6 m

EXTENSION

width limited by
zone of open space
in front of existing
window

existing
habitable
room

part of 'outer plane'
must be opposite part
of window

PLAN

3.6 m

(if H is not
more than 7.2 m)

Example B4

The limit on extension width in B3 need not apply if its roof is sufficiently low to fit under the 30° base plane of the 'zone of open space'.

3.6 m

(if H is not more
than 7.2 m)

SECTION

30°

1.2 m

ceiling height can be
less than 2300 mm if room
is not 'habitable'

EXTENSION

PLAN

habitable
room

EXTENSION

less
than
3.6 m

3.6 m

3.6 m

HOUSE EXTENSIONS AND STRUCTURAL FIRE PRECAUTIONS
Building Regulations Part E

Having found the limits (if any) on extension size in accordance with Part K, the next stage is to consider Part E requirements. These may determine the type of construction permitted and the size and position of any 'unprotected' areas in the external walls in relation to the 'Relevant boundary' (see definitions below).

'No change of use'
Extension of private house PG I: Part E applies to 'new work'; alterations and/or extensions. 'New work' must not adversely affect the 'existing'.

'Change of use'
Conversion from PG I to PG III into flats, maisonettes, etc. Part E applies to 'new work' (alterations and/or extensions) and also to the existing with the exception of the following (provided that the original building is not more than 3 storeys high — plus basement).

E7	External walls
E9 (6)	Compartment walls and compartment floors
E10 (4)	Protected shafts
E13	Stairways
E15	Restriction of surface flamespread over walls and ceilings.

Definitions:
Regulation E1 (1)
'Unprotected areas' in an external wall comprise the following (measured on elevation):

i Openings (eg windows, airvents, doors) but note that glass blocks are not 'unprotected areas' and that a door with fire resistance equal to that required for the wall and with an automatic self-closing device, is not an 'unprotected area'.*

ii Any part of the wall with fire resistance less than that specified in Regulation E5.

iii Any part with combustible cladding more than 1 mm thick, but note that if this is backed by a wall with the required fire resistance then the 'unprotected area' is taken as half the actual area of the combustible cladding.

'Relevant boundary' in relation to each side of a building is the actual site boundary (eg the centre-line of hedge, fence or wall) OR the centre line of an adjacent road or watercourse.

If a boundary is not parallel to the building, it can be 'relevant' to more than one side of the building — provided the angle between is not more than 80°:

*The reference to self-closing fire resistant doors is one of interpretation. The reader should note this for it may not be a universal one. Therefore any intention to consider a fire resistant door in an external wall as forming part of the fire resistant wall should be discussed with the Building Control Office before finalisation of designs.

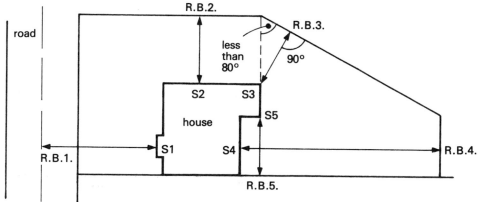

The distance between the relevant boundary (RB) and the side of the building (S) is measured at right angles to the RB.

The critical distance of 1 m from the RB might occur part way along an external wall, thus theoretically permitting a change of construction at this point but this would be awkward in practice.

The total of 'unprotected areas' permitted is directly related to the distance between an external wall and its relevant boundary: if this distance is less than 1 m (3 ft 3½ in) only the following areas are permitted:

Area A: not more than 1 m² (1556 in²)

Area B1, B2, B3 etc not more than 0.1 m² each (156 in²)

distance a not less than 4 m (13 ft 1½ in)

distance b not less than 1.5 m (4 ft 11 in)

(This is a diagrammatic elevation and does not indicate any limits of the actual positions of openings — other than the dimensions)

If the external wall is 1 m or more from the relevant boundary, the openings shown above are permitted, together with additional areas calculated by one of three methods, specified in Schedule 9 of the Building Regulations:

1 The enclosing rectangle
2 Aggregate notional area
3 Simplified method for small buildings in Purpose Groups I and III not more than 3-storeys high and not more than 24 m long.

The applicant can use whichever method gives the most favourable result. Methods 1 and 2 are fairly complicated. Method 3 is as follows:

| | Minimum distance from relevant boundary. | | | |
	1 m	2.5 m	5 m	6 m
Total Unprotected areas	5.6 m²	15 m²	Whole area of wall	
Length of side not exceding	24 m	24 m	12 m	24 m

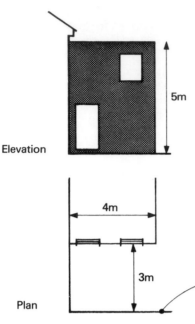

Elevation

Plan

4m

5m

3m

2 storey extension timber cladding on wall with ½ hour fire resistance.

Total wall area 5 x 4 = 20m²
including window 0.54m² }
and door   1.6m²   } 2.14m²

relevant boundary

Area of combustible cladding 20–2.14 = 17.86 m²
equivalent 'unprotected area' 17.86 ÷ 2 = 8.93 m²
(wall has required fire resistance)
∴ Total unprotected areas = 2.14 + 8.93 = 11.01 m²
From table (method 3) 15 m² is permitted more than 2.5 m from the relevant boundary: 11.01 m² is permitted therefore.

Example
As example 1, but 1.5 m from the relevant boundary. Using method 3, 5.6 m² total 'unprotected areas' permitted in external wall:
1 m to 2.5 m from RB
Window + door = 2.14 m²
       5.6–2.14 = 3.46 m²
∴ The maximum permitted area of combustible cladding (on a wall with the required period of fire resistance) is 3.46 x 2 = 6.92 m². If the window and door were omitted from this wall, the area of combustible cladding could be 5.6 x 2 = 11.2 m².

Unprotected areas on existing elevation

An existing external wall may be close to its relevant boundary (eg the side wall of a detached or semi-detached house). The requirements for 'unprotected areas' apply only to houses built after 1st February 1966, and it is totally acceptable for an older house to have elevations which do not comply with these requirements.

However, if an extension is added close to the same relevant boundary, the total elevation (existing + new) should not contravene the limits of unprotected areas up to the total limit OR if the 'existing' is above the limit then the new can have no unprotected areas except those permitted (see p103).

Example 3

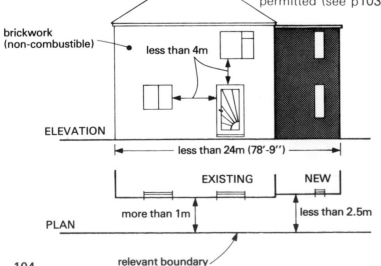

brickwork
(non-combustible)

less than 4m

ELEVATION

less than 24m (78'-9")

EXISTING   NEW

more than 1m   less than 2.5m

PLAN

relevant boundary

Existing windows and door 3.96 m²
Using method 3; 5.6 m² total unprotected areas permitted.
∴ the extension can have 5.6−3.96 = 1.64 m²
∴ 2 windows each 900 x 900 mm (total area 1.62 m²) are permitted, provided the cladding is non-combustible and the wall has the required fire resistance.
Note: the dimensions shown are for example only.

This new window is permitted (subject to Planning Approval) if less than 1 m² and more than 4 m from any other 'unprotected area' even if the existing openings exceed the permitted total 5.6 m² (method 3) provided the existing wall has non-combustible surface and the required period of fire resistance.

Example 4

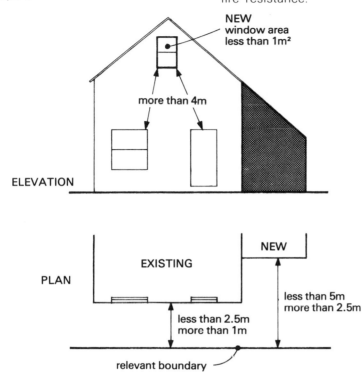

NEW
window area
less than 1m²

more than 4m

ELEVATION

PLAN

EXISTING

NEW

less than 5m
more than 2.5m

less than 2.5m
more than 1m

relevant boundary

The new external wall can be totally 'unprotected' if its area is less than 15 m² (ie it could be totally glazed, or have combustible cladding on a wall with no fire resistance).
Where the new external wall exceeds the permitted limits in relation to its relevant boundary, then the excess area must be protected — non-combustible cladding and fire resistance as follows:

A External wall 1 m or more from the relevant boundary
PG I house 1-, 2- or 3-storey extension — modified ½ hour fire resistance.
PG III building 1- or 2-storey extension — modified ½ hour fire resistance.
These periods of fire resistance are required from the inside only.

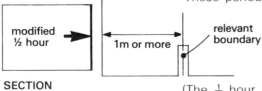

modified
½ hour

1m or more

relevant
boundary

SECTION

(The ½ hour period of fire resistance is modified to permit a rise in temperature on the external face, in excess of the limit specified in BS 476 after 15 minutes. This is taken into account in the constructions specified below).
Timber-frame external walls are permitted up to 3-storeys for (PG I house) and (PG III).
Schedule 8 Part 1 C4 in the Building Regulations lists deemed to satisfy constructions for timber frame external walls (non load bearing) more than 1 m from the relevant boundary (modified ½ hour fire resistance from inside only).

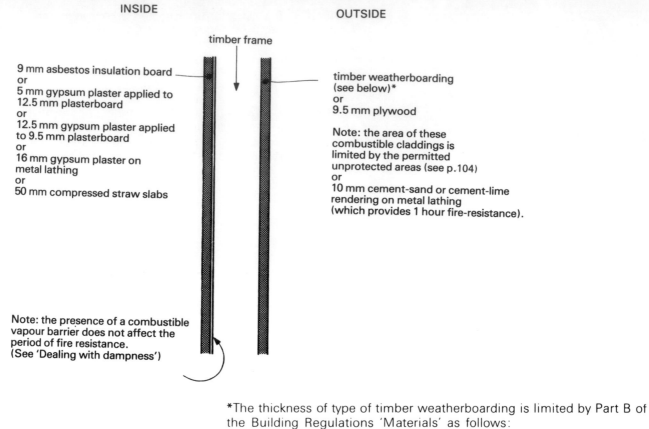

timber frame

9 mm asbestos insulation board
or
5 mm gypsum plaster applied to
12.5 mm plasterboard
or
12.5 mm gypsum plaster applied
to 9.5 mm plasterboard
or
16 mm gypsum plaster on
metal lathing
or
50 mm compressed straw slabs

timber weatherboarding
(see below)*
or
9.5 mm plywood

Note: the area of these
combustible claddings is
limited by the permitted
unprotected areas (see p.104)
or
10 mm cement-sand or cement-lime
rendering on metal lathing
(which provides 1 hour fire-resistance).

Note: the presence of a combustible
vapour barrier does not affect the
period of fire resistance.
(See 'Dealing with dampness')

*The thickness of type of timber weatherboarding is limited by Part B of
the Building Regulations 'Materials' as follows:
i the heartwood of 'durable' or 'very durable' timbers including tropical
hardwoods and two softwoods (western red cedar and sequoia) listed in
table 1 of Schedule 5.
or
ii 'moderately durable' or 'non-durable' timbers mainly softwoods but
with two hardwoods (abura and elm) listed in table 3 of Schedule 5,
provided the timber is preservative treated (as table 5 of Schedule 5),
and in either i or ii is not less than 16 mm thick or, in the case of
featheredge boarding, 16 mm at the thicker edge and 6 mm at the
thinner edge.
Certain wood-based sheet materials are permitted for external cladding:
plywood not less than 8 mm thick and of 'external' quality (ie 'ext WBP'
or marine grade)
hardboard — tempered hardboard to BS 1142: Part 2: 1971.
External walls more than 15 m high (49 ft 2½ in) are subject to more
stringent requirements (see Regulation E7).

B External wall less than 1 m from the relevant boundary
PG I house 1-, 2- or 3-storey extension — ½ hour fire resistance.
PG III building 1- or 2-storey extension — ½ hour fire resistance.

SECTION

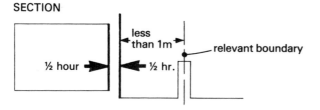

less
than 1m

relevant boundary

½ hour

½ hr.

These periods of fire resistance are required from each side.
Timber frame construction is permitted.
External cladding must when tested in accordance with
BS 476 Part 6 1968 'Fire propagation test for materials'
have an index of performance, I, not exceeding 12 and a sub-
index i_1 not exceeding 6.

Several deemed to satisfy constructions are listed in Schedule 8 Part 1 B5 for non-load-bearing timber frame external walls with ½ hour fire resistance from each side (see below). However, the only one of these which could be exposed externally (cement sand render on metal lathing) is not ideally suited to timber frame because of its wet application. Any of the others will require weatherproof external cladding (see 'comparative schedule of external cladding' attached to this chapter). Timber frame faced each side with 12.5 mm cement sand or gypsum plaster on metal lathing
or 5 mm gypsum plaster on 9.5 mm plasterboard
or 5 mm vermiculite plaster on 9.5 mm plasterboard
or 12.5 mm plasterboard
or 12.5 mm gypsum plaster on 12.5 mm fibre insulating board
or asbestos insulating board not less than 9 mm thick with 9 mm fillets to face of studs
or asbestos insulating board not less than 12 mm thick.
There is ample test evidence to show that wood-based sheet materials can provide fire protection to a timber frame equal to that provided by non-combustible materials (such as plasterboard or asbestos insulation board) and, unlike plasterboard or asbestos insulation board, can provide racking resistance to a timber frame: plywood, chipboard, hardboard or medium board are suitable for sheathing stud-frames or prefabricated framed panels.
Fire-test carried out at TRADA fire-testing laboratory 14th May, 1974.
Fire resistance of external wall panel (non-loadbearing).

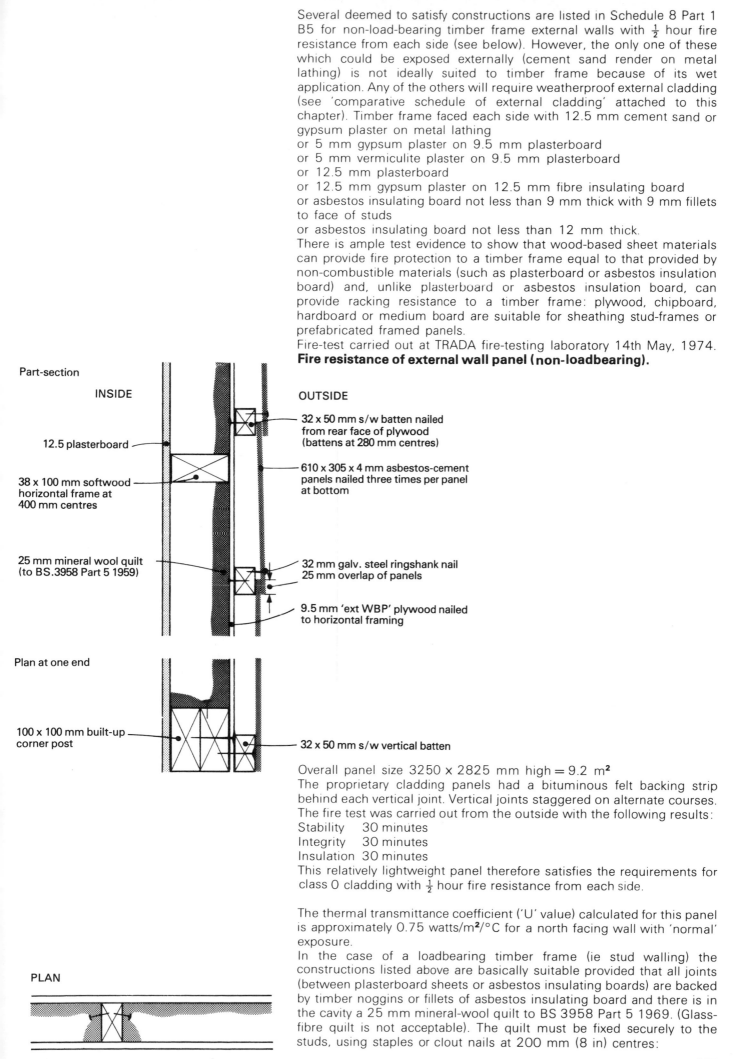

Part-section

INSIDE

OUTSIDE

12.5 plasterboard

32 x 50 mm s/w batten nailed from rear face of plywood (battens at 280 mm centres)

38 x 100 mm softwood horizontal frame at 400 mm centres

610 x 305 x 4 mm asbestos-cement panels nailed three times per panel at bottom

25 mm mineral wool quilt (to BS.3958 Part 5 1959)

32 mm galv. steel ringshank nail 25 mm overlap of panels

9.5 mm 'ext WBP' plywood nailed to horizontal framing

Plan at one end

100 x 100 mm built-up corner post

32 x 50 mm s/w vertical batten

Overall panel size 3250 x 2825 mm high = 9.2 m²
The proprietary cladding panels had a bituminous felt backing strip behind each vertical joint. Vertical joints staggered on alternate courses. The fire test was carried out from the outside with the following results:
Stability   30 minutes
Integrity   30 minutes
Insulation 30 minutes
This relatively lightweight panel therefore satisfies the requirements for class 0 cladding with ½ hour fire resistance from each side.

The thermal transmittance coefficient ('U' value) calculated for this panel is approximately 0.75 watts/m²/°C for a north facing wall with 'normal' exposure.
In the case of a loadbearing timber frame (ie stud walling) the constructions listed above are basically suitable provided that all joints (between plasterboard sheets or asbestos insulating boards) are backed by timber noggins or fillets of asbestos insulating board and there is in the cavity a 25 mm mineral-wool quilt to BS 3958 Part 5 1969. (Glass-fibre quilt is not acceptable). The quilt must be fixed securely to the studs, using staples or clout nails at 200 mm (8 in) centres:

PLAN

Several 'deemed to satisfy' constructions will be included in the proposed CP 112 Part 4 'Fire resistance of timber structures'.
Fire test carried out at TRADA firetesting laboratory 28th February, 1974.

Fire-resistance of external wall panel (load bearing)

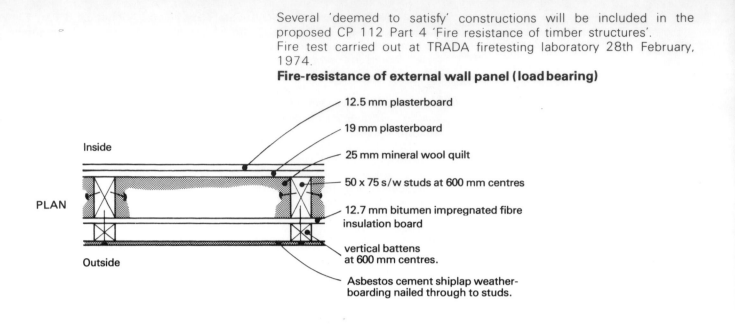

12.5 mm plasterboard

19 mm plasterboard

25 mm mineral wool quilt

50 x 75 s/w studs at 600 mm centres

12.7 mm bitumen impregnated fibre insulation board

vertical battens at 600 mm centres.

Asbestos cement shiplap weather-boarding nailed through to studs.

$\frac{1}{2}$ hour fire-resistance was achieved when tested from the outside. Note that the 19 mm layer of plasterboard is not necessary from the fire-resistance point of view. (Its presence in this construction was due to the client's desire to improve the sound insulation).
The timber studs were virtually undamaged at the end of the test.

REFERENCES

UK PARLIAMENT. The Building Regulations 1976. Statutory Instruments 1976, No 1676. London, HMSO. 1976.

BRITISH STANDARDS INSTITUTION. The structural use of timber: Part 2. Metric Units. British Standard Code of Practice CP 112: Part 2. London, BSI. 1971.

BRITISH STANDARDS INSTITUTION. Doors: Part 3. Fire-check flush doors and wood and metal frames (half-hour and one-hour type). British Standard BS 459: Part 3. London, BSI. 1951.

BRITISH STANDARDS INSTITUTION. Fire tests on building materials and structures: Part 6. Fire propagation test for materials. British Standard BS 476: Part 6. London, BSI. 1968.

BRITISH STANDARDS INSTITUTION. Fire tests on building materials and structures: Part 7. Surface spread of flame tests for materials. British Standard BS 476: Part 7. London, BSI. 1971.

BRITISH STANDARDS INSTITUTION. Timber grades for structural use. British Standard BS 4978. London, BSI. 1973.

BRITISH STANDARDS INSTITUTION. Fibre building boards: Part 2. Medium board and hardboard. British Standard BS 1142: Part 2. London, BSI. 1971.

FIBRE BUILDING BOARD DEVELOPMENT ORGANISATION. Fire-check doors. Technical Bulletin 11/72. London, FIDOR. 1972.

BURGESS, H.J. and MASTERS, M.A. Span charts for solid timber beams. Timber Research and Development Association, Publication TBL 34. Hughenden Valley, TRADA. 1976.

BURGESS, H.J. Introduction to the design of ply-web beams. Timber Research and Development Association, Information Bulletin E/IB/24. Hughenden Valley, TRADA. 1972.

BURGESS, H.J. Span tables for domestic purlins. Timber Research and Development Association, Information Bulletin E/IB/14. Hughenden Valley, TRADA. 1970.

BRITISH STANDARDS INSTITUTION. Thermal insulating materials: Part 5. Bonded mineral wool slabs (for use at temperatures above 50°C). British Standard BS 3958: Part 5. London, BSI. 1969.

BRITISH STANDARDS INSTITUTION. The structural use of timber: Part 4. Fire resistance of timber structures. British Standard BS 5268: Part 4. (Previously numbered CP 112: part 4) (To be published).

TIMBER RESEARCH AND DEVELOPMENT ASSOCIATION. Report of a fire resistance test performed on a section of external walling. Fire Test Report FR 167. TRADA, 28th February 1974. (Unpublished).

TIMBER RESEARCH AND DEVELOPMENT ASSOCIATION. Report of a fire resistance test carried out on an external wall assembly. Fire Test Report FR 176. TRADA, 14th May, 1974. (Unpublished).

NATIONAL HOUSE-BUILDING COUNCIL. Registered house-builder's handbook. London, NHBC. 1974.

BRITISH STANDARDS INSTITUTION. Recommendations for provision of space for domestic kitchen equipment. British Standard BS 3705. London, BSI. 1972.

ASHTON, L.A. Fire and timber in modern building design. Hughenden Valley, TRADA. Revised edition 1977.

HANDISYDE, C.C. Condensation in dwellings. Part 1: A design guide. Ministry of Public Buildings and Works. London, HMSO. 1970.

HANDISYDE, C.C. Condensation in dwellings. Part 2: Remedial measures. Department of the Environment. London, HMSO. 1971.

DEPARTMENT OF THE ENVIRONMENT. Spaces in the home: Bathrooms and WCs. Design Bulletin 24. Part 1. London, HMSO. 1972.

DEPARTMENT OF THE ENVIRONMENT. Spaces in the home: Kitchens and laundering spaces. Design Bulletin 24. Part 2. London, HMSO. 1972.

MINISTRY OF HOUSING AND LOCAL GOVERNMENT. Space in the home. Design Bulletin 6. (Metric) London, HMSO. 1968.

MINISTRY OF HOUSING AND LOCAL GOVERNMENT. Metrication of housebuilding. Circular 1/68. London, HMSO. 1968.

DEPARTMENT OF THE ENVIRONMENT. Public Health Act 1961: Building Regulations. Circular 67/71. London, HMSO. 1971.

Further Reading

TRADA Publications

Timber and the Building Regs. (1971).

Flame retardant treatments for timber. Wood Information, Section 2/3 Sheet 3. (1976).

Timber and wood-based sheet materials in fire. Wood Information, Section 4 Sheet 11. (1976).

Low flame spread wood based board products. Wood Information, Section 2/3 Sheet 7. (1977).

Watery Lane project. Reprint RSA 36. (1971).

Condensation. TRADA Library Bibliography TLB 129. 18 references (1976).

Vapour barriers. TRADA Library Bibliography TLB 062. 27 references (1978).

Plywood web beams. TRADA Library Bibliography TLB 056. 54 references (1978).

A comprehensive list of all TRADA's publication is available free on request.

Other Publications

BRITISH WOODWORKING FEDERATION. Guide to wood windows. Wood Information, Section 1 Sheet 8. London, BWF. 1977.

DEPARTMENT OF THE ENVIRONMENT. PROPERTY SERVICES AGENCY. Damp-proof courses and membranes. Advisory Leaflet 23. London, HMSO. 1976.

DEPARTMENT OF THE ENVIRONMENT. Dampness in buildings. Advisory Leaflet 47. London, HMSO. 1973.

BUILDING RESEARCH ESTABLISHMENT. Increasing the fire resistance of existing timber floors. Digest 208. London, HMSO. 1977.

BUILDING RESEARCH ESTABLISHMENT. Sound insulation of lightweight dwellings. Digest 187. London, HMSO. 1976.

EYKYN, B. All you need to know about loft conversions. Glasgow and London, Collins. 1975.

Index